# The Successful Management of Redundancy

## Human Resource Management in Action Series

*Edited by Brian Towers*

Successful Training Practice
*Alan Anderson*

Managing Performance Appraisal Systems
*Gordon Anderson*

European Employee Relations
*Jeff Bridgford and John Stirling*

Practical Employment Law
*Paul Lewis*

The Successful Management of Redundancy
*Paul Lewis*

Managing the Team
*Mick Marchington*

The Japanization of British Industry
*Nick Oliver and Barry Wilkinson*

Strategy and the Human Resource
*Ken Starkey and Alan McKinlay*

Handbook of Human Resource Management
*Edited by Brian Towers*

## Other HRM books from Blackwell Business

Successful Selection Interviewing
*Neil Anderson and Vivian Shackleton*

The Equal Opportunities Handbook
*Helen Collins*

Total Quality and Human Resources
*Barrie Dale and Cary Cooper*

The Handbook of Human Resource Planning
*Gordon McBeath*

Developments in the Management of Human Resources
*John Storey*

Women's Career Development
*Barbara White, Charles Cox and Cary Cooper*

# The Successful Management of Redundancy

PAUL LEWIS

BLACKWELL
*Business*

Copyright © Paul Lewis 1993

The right of Paul Lewis to be identified as author of this work has been asserted in accordance with the Copyright, Designs and Patents Act 1988.

First published 1993

First published in USA 1994

Blackwell Publishers
108 Cowley Road
Oxford OX4 1JF
UK

238 Main Street
Cambridge, Massachusetts 02142
USA

*British Library Cataloguing in Publication Data*
A CIP catalogue record for this book is available from the British Library.

*Library of Congress Cataloging-in-Publication Data*
Lewis, Paul, 1945–
    The successful management of redundancy/Paul Lewis.
        p.   cm. — (Human resource management in action series)
    'Blackwell business.'
    Includes bibliographical references and index.
    ISBN 0-631-18681-6 (pbk: alk. paper)
    1. Employees—Great Britain—Dismissal of.   2. Employees—Dismissal of—Law and legislation—Great Britain.   I. Title.   II. Series: Human resource management in action.
HF5549.5.D55L48   1994
658.3′134′0941—dc20
93-15322   CIP

Typeset in 11 on 13 pt Plantin by Best-set Typesetter Ltd., Hong Kong

This book is printed on acid-free paper by Page Bros
Norwich Ltd

*To Lew, Mina, Mary, Sarah and James*

# Contents

# List of Figures

# List of Tables

# Foreword

The growth in redundancies through the eighties and into the nineties has been mainly the product of the longest and deepest recession since the thirties. At the same time it is clear that organizations have been seeking to restructure, reorganize and remodel themselves to maximize efficiency – a process which was perhaps at its height in the middle to late eighties, and which is, to a degree, independent of the economic cycle. This search for a better utilization of resources has been primarily focused upon, and reflected in, staff reductions. Large-scale establishments employing several thousands are now much less evident and fast becoming objects of curiosity; and permanent, lifetime work with one employer now has to be virtually ruled out as the forces of competition, technology and rapidly obsolescing skills establish their dominion.

But how is all this to be managed? Once, in more innocent and less fraught times when trade unions were a major force and announcements of large-scale redundancies were greeted with astonishment followed by resistance, their principle of 'last in, first out' (LIFO) was all but mandatory and served social and political purposes if not economic and financial ones. Changed conditions have inevitably altered the rules. Managers now have much greater discretion, as ACAS observed in 1991 and again in 1992:

We noted in our Report last year that employers were increasingly seeking to make changes in the way they approached questions of selection for redundancy. That process continued in 1992, with further moves away from predetermined agreements that gave prime emphasis to last-in-first-out and more widespread attention to other criteria related to individual employment records, efficiency and contribution to the business. (ACAS Annual Report 1992, March 1993, p. 12.)

But if LIFO is now almost dead how can the 'other criteria' meet all the demands placed upon them? The answer is, with difficulty. As ACAS again has observed:

many situations in which we assisted during 1992 . . . had arisen between managements and unions about the criteria to be adopted for redundancy selection, and the way these should relate to particular groups of employees and individuals. (ACAS, pp. 12–13.)

Managers clearly need more charts and navigators to find a safer course through a redundancy exercise. Paul Lewis's book, written for managers, provides just that and even takes account of the 1992 European Community directive on collective redundancies. *If* redundancies are inevitable it is possible, as this book clearly demonstrates, to ensure that they 'contribute significantly to business goals, are acceptable to employees and meet the legal requirements'. All too rarely is this the case. This book should make it less so.

Brian Towers

# Preface

There is now no statutory code of practice to guide employers in the area of redundancy management, the 1972 Industrial Relations Code having been revoked. Yet the legal requirements remain, and in the recent recession (as in the early 1980s) the industrial tribunals were required to deal with an increasing number of claims in respect of unfair dismissal for redundancy and failure to consult with trades unions. The risk of falling foul of the legal requirements has been increased by the tendency of employers to move away from the mechanical last in, first out (LIFO) method of selection to criteria which more closely relate to business needs. This move is to be welcomed, but it does mean that employers are increasingly selecting people for redundancy in ways which may be less visible and more open to challenge. Moreover, the duties of employers in the area of redundancy are being increased as a result of new legislation required to give effect to the 1992 European Community directive on collective redundancies and to ensure full implementation of the 1975 directive.

*The Successful Management of Redundancy* aims to provide practical guidance for human resource managers in order to help them handle redundancies effectively, that is, without legal or industrial challenge. It adopts the manager's frame of reference and attempts to integrate law and good practice in addressing the various managerial issues which relate to redundancy. However, it is not a book that is simply about getting people out of the door quickly, quietly and cheaply. It also aims to demonstrate how employers may take a strategic approach to redundancy as part of the application of a wider human resource management philosophy, and how that strategy relates to the achievement of business goals. For example, redundancy is considered as an investment decision and attention is given to ways in which redundancy can be used to improve productivity and provide the company with a competitive edge in the market.

As part of taking both a practical, day-to-day and a wider, strategic view of the management of redundancy, *The Successful Management of Redundancy* deals with two issues which are commonly experienced by practitioners but largely overlooked by researchers and commentators. These are, first, the use of voluntary redundancy and, second, the question of how to minimize the problems of post-redundancy adjustment.

The Introduction sets redundancy within the context of human resource management. Part I of the book then deals with the options and strategies available to those who have to manage redundancy. Chapter 1 investigates the ways in which redundancy might be avoided or minimized. Chapter 2 considers the meaning of voluntary redundancy, how it can contribute to the achievement of organizational goals and the circumstances in which its deployment is likely to be most effective. The combination of voluntary redundancy and generous redundancy payments seems to have allowed industrial restructuring to proceed with minimal opposition in the 1980s and 1990s. Voluntary redundancy, arguably, is a significant as well as a widely-used technique in British employment relations. Chapter 3 examines the way in which redundancy can be used to improve business performance and chapter 4 considers a strategic approach to the management of redundancy.

Part II of the book is concerned with the legal framework. Chapter 5 deals with the definition of redundancy and chapter 6 with changes of employer. The remaining chapters – 7, 8 and 9 – cover unfair dismissal for redundancy, consultation with trades unions, and redundancy payments. The Conclusions provide an international view, and checklists for the management of redundancy are included as an appendix. A second appendix covers European Community initiatives including the 1992 directive on collective redundancies.

The term 'adjustment to market change' is used in the widest possible sense to refer to the policies of both public and private organizations, commercial or otherwise. The intention is to consider any situation where external events lead to a diminution in the demand for labour. Again, use of the word 'profitable' is intended to signify something broader than the conventional accounting measure, and 'business' and 'company' are not necessarily meant to imply the private sector.

It is recognized that less than 40 per cent of employees are members of trades unions. *The Successful Management of Redundancy*, therefore, does not assume a union presence, and is relevant to unionized and non-unionized situations alike. However, it does refer to union influences where these might occur and does recognize that problems in relation to redundancy may be greater where unions are present.

I shall feel I have succeeded if this book assists employers in devising and implementing redundancy strategies and policies which contribute significantly to business goals, are acceptable to employees and meet the legal requirements. This has been my objective and I wish to thank a number of people who have helped me try to achieve it. My thanks are due to the staff of the Advisory, Conciliation and Arbitration Service in Newcastle upon Tyne for reading the first draft and making helpful comments, and to the Editor of the *HRM in Action* series, Brian Towers, Professor of Industrial Relations at the University of Strathclyde. He drew on his wealth of editorial experience to provide advice which helped to shape and focus the work. He also read and made useful comments about the text and I am greatly indebted to him.

I am also indebted to Jane Steele of the Quayside Business Centre, Newcastle upon Tyne, and Norma Tuff for their first-class word processing; and to Maureen Parkin for co-ordinating the production of the script. I wish to thank the staff of Blackwell for compiling the index and the Controller of Her Majesty's Stationery Office for granting me permission to reproduce the Department of Employment's form for the advance notification of redundancies (below, pp. 121–2) and the redundancy payments ready reckoner (below, pp. 138–9).

The Trade Union Reform and Employment Rights Act received the Royal Assent in July 1993. Among other things, this amends the law as it relates to redundancy consultation, transfers of undertakings and unfair dismissal for redundancy. I have made some references to those amendments at appropriate points in the text.

There is also the question of changes in the statutory limits for redundancy, guarantee and insolvency payments. It should be noted that these are *not* being increased in 1993, although some limits, such as those relating to compensation for sex and race discrimination, were increased from 1 June. In recent years, limits for redundancy payments and other compensation have been increased annually on 1 April.

Finally the law is stated as at 1 March 1993 although some later developments have been included where this has proved possible.

Paul Lewis
Jesmond
Newcastle upon Tyne

# List of Abbreviations

| | |
|---|---|
| AC | Appeal Cases Reports |
| ACAS | Advisory, Conciliation and Arbitration Service |
| All ER | All England Reports |
| anor | Another (in the names of legal cases) |
| BCE | British Coal Enterprise |
| BT | British Telecom plc |
| c. | Chapter (in relation to statutes) |
| CA | Court of Appeal |
| CAC | Central Arbitration Committee |
| CMLR | Common Market Law Reports |
| CS | Court of Session |
| DE | Department of Employment |
| EAT | Employment Appeal Tribunal |
| EC | European Community |
| ECJ | European Court of Justice |
| EDT | Effective date of termination |
| EGP | *Ex gratia* payment |
| EPA | Employment Protection Act 1975 |
| EP(C)A | Employment Protection (Consolidation) Act 1978 |
| ETO | Economic, technical or organizational reason (for dismissal arising out of the transfer of an undertaking) |
| FHEA | Further and Higher Education Act 1992 |
| GPMU | Graphical, Paper and Media Union |
| HL | House of Lords |
| HMSO | Her Majesty's Stationery Office |
| HRM | Human resource management |
| HSC | Health and Safety Commission |
| HSE | Health and Safety Executive |
| ICR | Industrial Cases Reports |

| | |
|---|---|
| ICTA | Income and Corporation Taxes Act 1988 |
| IDS | Incomes Data Services |
| IMS | Institute of Manpower Studies |
| IPM | Institute of Personnel Management |
| IRLIB | Industrial Relations Legal Information Bulletin |
| IRLR | Industrial Relations Law Reports |
| IRS | Industrial Relations Services |
| IT | Industrial tribunal |
| ITR | Industrial Tribunal Reports |
| LIFO | Last in, first out |
| NALGO | National and Local Government Officers' Association |
| NATFHE | National Association of Teachers in Further and Higher Education |
| NHS | National Health Service |
| NI | National Insurance |
| NIRC | National Industrial Relations Court |
| NRA | Normal retiring age |
| NUM | National Union of Mineworkers |
| OECD | Organisation for Economic Co-operation and Development |
| OJ | Official Journal (of the EC) |
| ors | Others (in the names of legal cases) |
| PAYE | Pay as you earn (taxation) |
| R | Regina (in the names of legal cases) |
| RP | Redundancy payment |
| s. | Section (of a statute) |
| SDA | Sex Discrimination Act (1975, 1986) |
| SI | Statutory instrument |
| SOSR | Some other substantial reason (for dismissal) |
| ss. | Sections (of a statute) |
| SSCBA | Social Security Contributions and Benefits Act 1992 |
| T/A | Trading as |
| TUC | Trades Union Congress |
| TULR(C)A | Trade Union and Labour Relations (Consolidation) Act 1992 |
| TURERA | Trade Union Reform and Employment Rights Act 1993 |
| UCTA | Unfair Contract Terms Act 1977 |
| UK | United Kingdom |
| VR | Voluntary redundancy |
| WLR | Weekly Law Reports |

# Introduction

The development of human resource management (HRM) in the UK has given rise to much debate.[1] In particular, researchers and commentators have been concerned to identify its key components, to establish whether it is qualitatively different from previous approaches to the management of people, to determine how far it has been implemented in practice and to consider its implications.

It seems that HRM is likely to start from the view that people are a significant source of potential for an organization, and that the way they are managed ultimately may affect that organization's ability to compete in the marketplace. It follows from this view of the employee as an asset that HRM implies a strong focus upon the individual. This might lead to an individual rather than a collective approach to communication as well as to a greater emphasis on the individual's work and rewards. The stronger focus on individual performance may mean that appraisal and development assume more prominence in the personnel function. These sorts of features perhaps indicate an attempt to integrate the individual into the organization on the basis of commitment rather than compliance, and may imply an organic and devolved structure rather than a bureaucratic and centralized one.

An important feature of HRM seems to be the adoption of a strategic approach and the linking of this strategy to overall business objectives. Such an approach implies a coherent set of personnel policies which are integrated with line management functions and are demonstrably in support of organizational goals. A prerequisite of this may be the presence of the HRM function at board level.

It can be argued that viewing the employee as a resource to be developed rather than as a cost to be minimized will lead to an emphasis upon the soft aspects of people management, such as training and development, rather than upon the hard areas, such as discipline and redundancy.[2] However, the soft dimension has to be set alongside the need for HRM to be firmly anchored in the organization's objectives. This may result in the hard aspects of HRM coming to the fore, involving cost-cutting and redundancies. Possibly, these hard and soft approaches may be different aspects of one strategy, which some have called 'tough love'.[3] Here a positive approach to matters such as appraisal, development and rewards exists alongside a determination to tackle barriers to business success, such as the existence of incompetent and/or surplus staff. An alternative way of reconciling the hard and the soft is to conclude that the best business results are obtained by developing the potential of employees in order to secure the output of high quality products or services.

HRM is a relatively recent phenomenon in the UK and researchers are uncertain about its nature and significance. What is fairly clear, however, is that a HRM approach to the management of people does not preclude the occurrence of redundancy. Indeed, in as much as it encourages the 'tough love' approach it actually may *result* in redundancy. On the other hand, an organization which values its people might be expected to engage in a certain amount of manpower planning and retraining, both of which may have the effect of reducing the incidence of redundancy. Above all, however, HRM suggests that managers will take a strategic approach to redundancy, and be proactive rather than reactive.

What might this involve? Certainly, it will involve forming a view about whether the organization's level of staffing is in keeping with its turnover and financial results. From this might flow policies for redundancy and/or redundancy avoidance or minimization. Where redundancy is considered necessary, a strategic approach would include regarding redundancy as an investment and using it as a vehicle for securing organizational improvements. Next, the strategy might aim to minimize the disruption which can arise from redundancy, whether from union opposition or post-redundancy dislocation. It could also assist the organization in preserving its good name, since this might affect staff recruitment, retention and commitment, as well as sales. Finally, a strategic approach to redundancy would aim to minimize the likelihood of infringement of the law and legal challenges. This might be part of a wider policy seeking to ensure that the organization's managers perform their roles in ways which limit exposure to litigation and prosecution.

The legal framework for redundancy is provided by part II of this book. It deals with the definition of redundancy, changes of employer, unfair dismissal for redundancy, consultation with trades unions and redundancy payments. Part I is concerned with the options and strategies open to those who have to manage redundancy. It addresses the general question of redundancy strategy as well as specific aspects such as business performance and voluntary redundancy. First of all, however, it considers the preliminary matter of how management might respond to market change.

## Notes

1 See, for example, Storey, J., (Ed.) *New Perspectives on Human Resource Management*, London: Routledge, 1991; Guest, D.E., Human Resource Management and Industrial Relations, *Journal of Management Studies*, Vol. 24, No. 5, 1987, pp. 503–22; and Towers, B., (Ed.) *The Handbook of Human Resource Management*, Oxford: Blackwell, 1992.
2 Storey, J., Introduction: From Personnel Management to Human Resource Management, in Storey, *New Perspectives*, pp. 1–18, see p. 8.
3 Legge, K, Human Resource Management: A Critical Analysis, in Storey, *New Perspectives*, pp. 19–40, see p. 32.

# Part I

# Managing Redundancy: Options and Strategies

# 1

# Responding to Market Change

## The Avoidance of Redundancy

Redundancy is a response to market change, but is it the only, or most appropriate response? Can redundancy be avoided, and if so, should it be? An organization may face a diminished demand for labour because of a short-term or long-term decline in product sales, because of a need for immediate and/or long-term cost savings or because of the introduction of new technology. Indeed, a combination of these factors may be present.

A major consideration is whether a reduced wages bill is seen as necessary. This is likely to depend on the scale of any savings needed, opportunities for savings in other areas (for example, materials, overheads, stocks or services), measures of labour productivity and the scope for technological change. If overstaffing is perceived as an element in the problem a reduced demand for labour is likely. In theory, however, the need for financial savings and increased productivity does not *require* a reduced demand for labour. New working practices, improved capital utilization and increased capitalization are examples of other possible responses. Unfortunately, the time-scale during which savings need to be effected is often too short for companies to rely on such measures alone. In practice, therefore, it is likely that a range of policies, including a reduced demand for labour, will be used and this will be particularly so where the competitiveness of the firm needs substantial improvement. Cost reduction measures accompanied by price cuts may offer, however, only a short-term competitive advantage if they result in reduced investment in training, technology, research and development, since long-term competitiveness may be hampered. Where the market (or market share) has already shrunk, there is clearly a direct link between a diminution in product demand and a reduction in the demand for labour since the latter is derived from the former, but as with cost-cutting, this does not mean that redundancies are inevitable. Other options may be available, for example, labour hoarding.

An important distinction here is between *permanent* changes in labour demand leading to redundancy and *temporary* ones which do not, and which are typically absorbed out of profits. In the latter case the enterprise can be seen as making an investment by employing more people than it needs. This is an investment in staff retention to avoid the high cost of future labour adjustment (recruitment, training etc.). It can also be seen as an investment in staff loyalty, but at a certain point the ability to sustain such investment may cease because the likelihood of ever returning to the previous employment level has receded. In such circumstances, redundancy becomes more likely.

An organization's ability to avoid redundancy is likely to depend in part upon the effectiveness of its human resource planning. If such planning has been done properly there should be early warning of likely staff surpluses and an opportunity to pursue policies to avoid redundancy, such as the placing of restrictions upon recruitment and the retraining of surplus staff to enable them to fill the vacancies created through natural wastage. Organizational response is also likely to depend upon existing flexibility, particularly in relation to jobs and locations. The more flexibility here, the greater the scope for redeployment.

The policies most commonly adopted in order to avoid redundancy, in the context of a reduced demand for labour, are described below. They can be seen as constituting a marketing approach or a manpower reaction.[1] The former focuses upon improved market performance, for example, by developing new markets, or by being more competitive in existing markets. The latter concentrates on adjusting labour supply without the need for redundancy, and includes natural wastage, work sharing, early retirement, redeployment and labour hoarding.

## Types of Adjustment

An employer may be able to avoid redundancy altogether, or at least reduce the number, by adopting one or more of the policies described below. For example, natural wastage, restriction of recruitment, incentives for early retirement and the use of work sharing may form a useful combination.

## Labour hoarding

Employers may retain employees even if they have a reduced demand for labour. This occurred in Britain in the 1950s and 1960s in a period of full employment. Firms were anxious about their ability to respond to market upturns if they made employees redundant during temporary recessions. Similar concerns might apply even in a period of unemployment if certain categories of worker are in short supply. Hoarding is likely to be economically feasible only as a means of dealing with short-term problems, especially if normal hours of work and production are maintained but with surplus output going to stocks. However, labour hoarding could be used in conjunction with work sharing and/or other policies.

## Wage reduction and/or productivity improvement

Economic analysis suggests that a reduction in wages will lead to an increased demand for labour. Where the market problem is mostly to do with relatively high unit costs and a lack of competitiveness, a reduced demand for labour may be averted by this means. Increased labour productivity also may be important.

## Natural wastage and a freeze on recruitment

It may be possible to reduce the size of the workforce through a policy of not replacing leavers. Surplus employees may then be transferred to the vacant posts. This policy is likely to be suitable where a long-term reduction in staff is required and:

- the company's difficulties are not such as to demand large and immediate reductions;
- there is an ability to carry the costs of excess staff until a productive role is found for those staff; and
- the rate of labour turnover is high enough to make the exercise possible within an acceptable period of time.

However, restricting recruitment will eventually distort the structure of the workforce and reduce the supply of people with promotion potential. Natural wastage will also cause distortions and will become less effective as turnover is likely to be lower among an increasingly long-serving workforce.

## Retirement policy

Those employees already beyond normal retiring age could be required to retire, and incentives provided for early retirement. Typically, the latter would require enhancement of pensionable service if it was to be attractive (see below, pp. 149–50). A major consideration with use of early retirement will be to ensure that the retained workforce is adequate (in terms of size, skills, experience etc.) to meet operational requirements (see chapter 3).

## Retraining and transfers

There is a possibility of retraining and transfer to other parts of the firm especially if the firm is large and diverse and the factors which have caused a fall in the demand for labour are not universal. For example, large-scale transfers were possible in the past in the British coal and steel industries as some areas declined and new ones opened up. In Japan and Germany (formerly West Germany) retraining and transfer is a commonly used form of internal adjustment in larger firms. When using this method of adjustment, employers will need to take into account the terms of the contracts of employment of their employees.

## Work sharing

A reduced demand for labour may be effected by reducing the hours of work of employees while leaving the number of employees unchanged. Hourly rates of pay would not be altered except in as much as premium working time was reduced. Work sharing may be ad hoc, that is, a specific response to a temporary problem. In such cases the aim might be to reduce or eliminate overtime and extra shifts so that the company can retain its surplus staff. Another possibility is the introduction of short-time working, such as a three or four day week, although the terms of employment contracts and any possible industrial relations effects will need to be borne in mind. However, the problem may be one which requires a per-manent reduction in the size of the workforce, and an ongoing, systematic response. In such circumstances, it may be feasible to use a combination of work sharing and natural wastage, so that leavers are not replaced and surplus labour is absorbed over a longer period. Reductions in the length of working week, working year or even working life may assist the process but the reduction of overtime (and the removal of temporary staff) may restrict management's ability to meet its staffing needs.

### Termination or reduction of contracts for services

Adjustment may be made by terminating or reducing contracts for services (cleaning, catering etc.). This will not lead to redundancies in the firm making the adjustment, but may lead to redundancies in the contracting firms. This would not necessarily be the case however, especially if the firms had other contracts under which the displaced workers might be employed. The degree of flexibility here would be influenced by the terms of the contracts, and in particular by the provisions for termination.

This approach draws on the concept of the flexible firm, where labour adjustments are made through the peripheral labour force (contractors, the self-employed, agency staff etc.) rather than through the core of permanent employees.

### Improving market share

A firm may seek to respond to a diminished demand for labour, because, for example, of a lack of competitiveness, by a whole range of marketing initiatives. New products may be introduced, or existing ones developed. Quality of product, customer liaison and after-sales service might be improved. Other aspects of the marketing function, for example, market research, sales or distribution might be strengthened. Much depends upon the diagnosis of what is wrong. If unit costs are out of line, increased use of capital may be part of the solution. If labour productivity is a problem, changes in working practices may be part of the answer. This approach looks to avoid a reduced demand for labour by increasing the firm's market share.

### Temporary and/or partial closures and lay-offs

Finally, the only method of avoiding redundancy may be the temporary closure of some or all of the operation and the laying off of employees. This has the drawbacks of loss of revenue, temporariness of savings and restart costs. Also, it may lead to employees claiming in contract or under statute (the latter in respect of deductions under the Wages Act 1986 or for a redundancy payment (RP) under the Employment Protection (Consolidation) Act 1978 (EP(C)A) lay-off provisions, see below, pp. 131–3).

## Determining the Response

Four groups of factors may be seen as influencing which policies are adopted: workforce attributes, company characteristics, the market situation and employment relations.

### Workforce attributes

The attitudes of employees may play a part in determining the options available to management. Attitudes towards wage reductions, flexible working and transfer to other locations could be instrumental in determining whether or not there is going to be a redundancy. Attitudes towards early retirement and redundancy may be significant. Unions may prefer redundancies to wage reductions in order to defend wage rates in the trade or industry, especially if members can retire early with a good financial deal.

Structural factors may be an influence. These include the age structure of the workforce, length of employment, skills, experience, pay and status. Industry or company-specific skills and experience limited to one firm or industry may discourage employee adaptation to new circumstances. Where pay and status are high in the original jobs, retraining and transfer may be more difficult to achieve.

### Company characteristics

The firm's profit record and reserves affect the ability to pay for solutions to its market problem. Opposition to redundancy can probably be bought out through redundancy payments and generous early pension arrangements. Other solutions, such as labour hoarding, may also be expensive.

Whether a firm is public or private may affect the options which are available. Governments may wish to avoid redundancies for political reasons. They may fund losses which would lead to insolvency or takeover if they occurred in the private sector. On the other hand, governments may wish to encourage redundancy for economic restructuring purposes. In fact, some of the largest-scale redundancies have taken place in publicly-owned industries in order to achieve such restructuring (for example, railways, shipbuilding, coal and steel).

Another characteristic which may be important is production flexibility. This refers to the freedom enjoyed by the firm in making changes to production plans, capital/labour ratios and technology in the short-term. The greater the flexibility here, the more likely that adjustment to market change will be easier, and that redundancy can be avoided.

An organization's overall employment policy will be of importance. Many employment relationships are long and stable. Employees give loyalty and long-term commitment in exchange for the employer acting in good faith by using proper procedures where applicable and not adversely varying the terms of employment. This goes a long way towards explaining why employers did not generally try to cut wages in the 1980s despite the availability of a pool of unemployed people who might have been prepared to work for lower wages, and despite government exhortation to search for wage flexibility.

One of the influences at work is the time-scale a firm will take to assess the costs and benefits of its employment policies. Thus, a short-term perspective may show wage cuts to be an attractive option. A longer-term view would have to build in costs associated with lower morale and staff loss and replacement.

Extent and choice of options may also be influenced by the labour turnover rate, the extent of contracted-out work and the company's desired image.

### The market situation

The options available will be limited if the company is seriously out of line with its main competitors as regards unit costs. In such circumstances it will be looking for savings across the board and it would be surprising if some redundancies did not occur. This was probably the paradigm case of the 1980s, at least in the traditional manufacturing sector. Responses usually included changed working practices and reduced staffing levels.

An important influence upon the options available in response to a market problem is whether the problem is cyclical or structural. A reduced demand for labour because of a temporary recession offers more possibilities of avoiding redundancy than does one occurring because of long-term structural factors. Excess capacity can be retained in the short term ready for an upturn, but cannot be used if there is a long-term decline.

## Employment relations

In a unionized setting, there may be existing rules governing redundancy procedures (for example, selection; use of voluntary redundancy; consultation) and limits in practice as to how far the firm can depart from these, if at all. The same may be true of redundancy terms (redundancy payments; pension arrangements etc.). Some aspects of terms and procedures may be determined outside the organization, for instance, by industry-wide agreements.

In large multi-plant firms different aspects of the response may take place at different levels. Productivity negotiations may need to take place locally, as may the operation of any voluntary redundancy scheme, but the local industrial relations parties may find that much of the direction of the response has been decided at a higher level. That leaves their main job as implementation of what has already been decided. Employees still may have the choice of staying or going, and the local union may have a residual power to take industrial action, but these are unlikely to disturb the direction of the response of a large firm, which in any case may have been agreed with unions at company level.

Governments often determine some of the procedural and substantive minima in this area. Legal rules about consultation, selection and levels of payment impose some restraints on the firm. On the other hand, legislation allows redundancy as a legitimate action providing that the legal rules have been followed.

## Redundancy as an Investment Decision

In many cases the economic and other aspects of adjustment to change will point employers towards redundancy rather than other responses. First, it will be difficult to avoid redundancy where very large productivity increases and cost savings are required. Maintaining surplus employees in post does not make sense (at least in the short term) if the aim is to secure cost savings to allow the firm to compete more effectively. Second, redundancy is likely to be a popular policy among employees where there is an ageing workforce and the possibility of early retirement with enhanced pensionable years. This will be so especially where voluntary redundancy is to be used. Third, redundancy will be difficult to avoid where the whole company (and perhaps industry) is in decline. Cost savings are likely to be needed and the chances of redeployment limited. Finally, redundancy may be more likely where flexibility has been resisted in the past by a strong trades union. Lack of flexibility in the past may mean that the possibilities for avoiding redundancy (for example, by using redeployment) are reduced although the scope for flexibility may be greater. Moreover, management may favour redundancy because they see it as providing an opportunity to introduce the flexibility they need.

Overall, employers may be able to take a cost/benefit approach to the different forms of adjustment. For example, the costs of lay-offs and/or short-time working (such as those deriving from any contractual and/or statutory liabilities) can be set against the savings which accrue, and the outcome may be compared with that produced from a similar exercise applied to other forms of adjustment. An important advantage of redundancy, in this respect, is the opportunity it provides for the introduction of change. Redundancy can be seen as an investment decision where once-for-all costs (such as redundancy payments) yield a stream of continued savings through increased productivity and other improvements (see chapter 3). Redundancy, where the voluntary redundancy technique is used, is also likely to permit a relatively speedy response when compared with the protracted negotiations which may be necessary to achieve other forms of adjustment such as wage reductions. However, as noted in chapter 2, voluntary redundancy is likely to require a substantial investment because of the need to have a level of RP high enough to bring forth volunteers.

In a unionized setting, the costs of different options may be influenced by the policies adopted by the union. For example, a policy of opposition to redundancy adopted by a strong union may give an impetus to other types of solution. Also, where a union succeeds in negotiating a high level of RP, other strategies (such as labour hoarding) might become more attractive to management. Similarly, acceptance of lower wages effectively trades job losses for wage reductions. This last point indicates that a union may be able to influence management's choice of option even if it has little bargaining power *vis-à-vis* management. This is because the relative costs of the different forms of management action can be changed by the union *reducing* the cost of some of them as well as by it increasing the cost of others.

## Note

1  W.W. Daniel, The United Kingdom, in M. Cross, (Ed.), *Managing Workforce Reduction*, London: Croom Helm Ltd, 1985, p. 75.

# 2
# The Voluntary Redundancy Option

Voluntary redundancy (VR) has become widely used as a method of dealing with redundancy, but what are the advantages of adopting it and under what conditions will it be most effective? Does it have any disadvantages, and what can be done to increase the supply of volunteers if there is a shortfall? These are the questions now addressed. The starting point is an investigation into what is meant by voluntary redundancy: neither law nor practice has defined the term precisely.

## The Meaning of Voluntary Redundancy

In both law and practice redundancy is defined as a situation in which an employer dismisses employees because he or she requires fewer of them. The reason for this reduced demand for labour does not affect whether the situation created is or is not a redundancy, and it is established law and practice that a diminution in the amount of work to be done is not a prerequisite. A redundancy can occur with an unchanged workload if an employer seeks to reduce unit costs through decreased staffing.

At first sight, the fact that redundancy is a form of dismissal seems to present a problem in relation to voluntary redundancy; termination agreed by both parties is regarded as mutual termination and not as dismissal. However, examination of the nature of the VR bargain shows how voluntary redundancy and the act of dismissal are compatible. The agreement would not occur without the offer of a redundancy payment (RP) from the employer, and the offer of voluntary acceptance of redundancy by the employee. The bargain does not amount to a termination because neither party is notifying termination. It is a promissory bargain, in which the employer promises to make a RP and the employee promises to accept dismissal on grounds of redundancy. It can be seen as a contract based on an offer to dismiss with a RP in exchange for the employee voluntarily relinquishing his or her job (that is, agreeing to be dismissed). The voluntary redundancy contract provides for acceptance of dismissal on agreed terms. Thus, there is a dismissal, notwithstanding the fact that it is agreed beforehand, and this feature helps to distinguish VR from early retirement, which is normally a mutual termination.[1]

An important aspect of the VR agreement is that no individual employee is compelled to enter into it. Among all employees to whom the VR scheme applies there is a choice between being made redundant and not being made redundant. This characteristic distinguishes VR from compulsory redundancy, where a named individual employee is made redundant regardless of his or her wishes. It follows that with voluntary redundancy the individual employee has some influence over the redundancy decision, although the individual's choice may be circumscribed to a greater or lesser degree by the context in which the redundancies occur.

Employees (and union officials) tend to see redundancy as voluntary only if the employee can remain in something like his or her own job. The belief that an employee acquires property rights in the job provides a philosophical basis for this approach. By contrast, the essential ingredient in VR as far as management is concerned is likely to be the possibility of the employment contract continuing. An employer's concern will be to sustain only that employment which is profitable, and to ensure labour flexibility as a means to that end. Therefore, there may be strongly divergent views about what is meant by voluntary redundancy, with employees stressing *job* continuity and employers focusing upon *employment* continuity. It follows that there is no universally accepted definition of voluntary redundancy other than one which states that the individual has a choice. Whether any particular redundancy can be defined as voluntary will depend in part upon the perspective adopted.

On the collective front, any VR agreement with a union can be seen as offering enhanced payments to union members in exchange for union acquiescence in the redundancies. Unions and their members often oppose redundancies on the grounds that an employee has a property right in the job, this being acquired through long service. An employer may make enhanced payments through VR to avoid costs being imposed by employees acting in concert to defend their perceived job rights. As is noted in the next section, VR can be used in a unionized setting to transfer redundancy decision-making from the collective bargaining process to the individual level. This is one of a number of features of VR which may contribute significantly to the achievement of organizational goals.

## Reasons for Adopting the Voluntary Redundancy Technique

### Motivational and facilitating factors

A distinction can be drawn between the reasons why VR may be adopted as policy (that is, how it helps to meet the employer's objectives) and the circumstances in which its deployment may be most effective (that is, why it works in practice). The former may be regarded as motivational factors, the latter as facilitating ones. (See below, pp. 25–7, in respect of the facilitating factors.)

### Cost-effectiveness

The economic basis of the motivational factors is that VR is cost-effective, that is, the costs of VR are less than the costs which are perceived as likely under compulsory redundancy. There are two influences at work here. First, under compulsory redundancy unions and/or individual employees may impose costs upon employers by defending jobs. Therefore, management may use VR to avoid the conflict which might be caused by compulsory redundancy and resultant union and/or employee action. The use of VR is likely to reduce the chances of industrial action being taken and unfair dismissal claims being pursued. The adoption of VR may be particularly beneficial where redundancies are proposed on a large scale, where there could be a significant effect on the local economy or where union organization is strong.

Second, corporate image or reputation may be damaged by the use of compulsory redundancy. The reasons for a concern with image may be found in possible effects upon the recruitment of staff, product sales and staff loyalty, commitment and retention. Use of compulsory redundancy may hinder the recruitment of qualified staff and if the organization is in a high turnover and therefore high recruitment sector (such as retailing) the effect could be costly. A second possibility is that corporate image is part of the marketing of products. Thus, quality of product is enhanced by the general company image, including how the firm handles staff relations. Poor quality employment relations, especially if publicly visible, may have costs in terms of reduced consumer demand because consumers begin to doubt the quality of the company's products. Corporate image may be particularly important for firms with national or international reputations, for firms where quality of product is important or where a firm has a high profile in the local community. Use of compulsory redundancy may also be detrimental to the morale of existing staff. They are likely to view VR as a more positive approach to the problem of labour surplus, since it gives employees a choice and increases the opportunities for early retirement, including early retirement on ill-health grounds.

In the public sector there may be a concern with image because of a wish not to antagonize political masters. Indeed, political masters may dictate that compulsory redundancy be avoided out of fear of loss of popularity and consequent loss of political support. The leaders of public bodies may also subscribe to a belief that public organizations should set a good example, that is, follow an implicit code of good practice.

Where redundancy is a cost-saving exercise, it represents an investment by management. Once-for-all payments are made in order to secure continued savings in labour costs. Voluntary redundancy enables the investment to be made with a minimum of harmful effects and by doing so keeps down the cost of that investment.

### Reduced opposition to redundancies

Voluntary redundancy may result in reduced opposition to redundancy for three reasons. First, the VR process may weaken a union's bargaining position. This is because the union membership becomes divided between those wishing to accept VR and those wishing to protect jobs – so that the unity of purpose necessary for effective opposition is not achieved. Moreover, because management will have in their possession the list of volunteers, the extent of the union's division will be known. Those wishing to accept VR may be reluctant to support industrial action. At the very least, a union is likely to be uncertain about the support it might obtain from its members if action were sought. In as much as union officials follow their union's formal policy of opposition to redundancy, there may be tensions between officials and members if a substantial proportion of the latter wish to accept VR, although some members may well oppose VR on the grounds that jobs are lost even though nobody is forcibly dismissed.

Secondly, VR makes the redundancy decision individual rather than collective. The potentially problematic collective decision is replaced by a number of individual employee decisions which are much more amenable to management influence. (This is presented diagrammatically in figure 1.) VR may be seen as a technique through which management controls conflict by fragmenting it. It emphasizes employee/employer harmony and enhances employee and employer influence at the expense of union influence. It encourages non-militant behaviour on the part of employees by giving the individual not only more influence but also the prospect of an acceptable

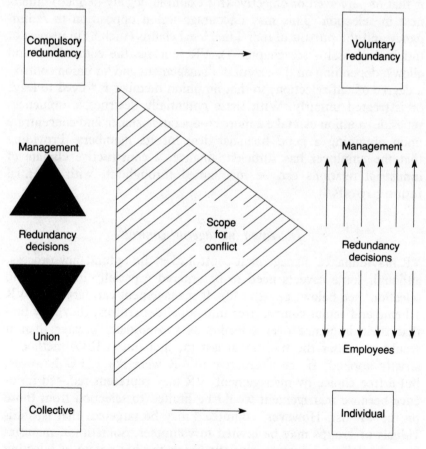

A unionized workplace is assumed

**Figure 1** Voluntary redundancy and the individualization of redundancy decisions

alternative to continued employment. The above development can be seen as representing an extension of the freedom to contract by allowing employees and employers to contract with each other over an issue which, in unionized workplaces, would normally be settled through collective bargaining.

The third reason for VR resulting in reduced opposition to redundancy is that it may help to solve two important problems often associated with redundancy. One of these is the problem of compulsion, which may encourage considerable union opposition. In practice, many unions do not oppose redundancy *per se* because they regard technological and market change as facts of life; however, they *do* oppose hard (that is, compulsory) redundancy. The other problem is that of perceived or objective (for example, legally-defined) unfairness in selection. This may encourage union opposition to redundancy and the pursuit of individual legal claims (such as in respect of unfair dismissal – see chapter 7). VR removes the compulsion and allows, depending on the extent of management and/or union control, a degree of self-selection, so that no union member is forced to leave or is treated unfairly. With these potentially destructive influences set aside, a union can take a more co-operative stance and concentrate upon obtaining a good financial deal for its members. Providing that the employer has sufficient finance, a constructive climate of industrial relations can be maintained throughout, with potential future pay-offs.

### Increased managerial control

VR may enhance management control over the redundancy process, although some caveats need to be entered especially in relation to selection (see below, pp. 28–30). If management can target the VR scheme and retain control over individual departures, they may find that their influence over selection is substantially greater than it would be under the traditional last in, first out (LIFO) method if strictly applied. If the alternative to VR were not LIFO however, but a free choice by management, VR may represent reduced influence because management would be limited to selection from those on the VR list. However, volunteers may be targeted, that is, individuals or groups may be invited to volunteer. Sometimes, management have been happy to give the union the hot potato of selecting from the pool of volunteers. On occasions this has resulted in unions being criticized by members whose redundancy was delayed or prevented by the union's selection. It should be noted that the use of VR in itself is not likely to be regarded as a customary selection arrangement under Section 59 of the EP(C)A (see chapter 7). On the facts in *Rogers and ors* v. *Vosper Thorneycroft (UK) Ltd*, VR was held to be a device for creating a pool of volunteers from which selection was to be made.

Another way in which VR may facilitate increased managerial control over the redundancy process is by encouraging direct communication with employees. Voluntary redundancy supposes such communication because the decision to volunteer and the decision to allow a particular volunteer to go relate to the individual employment relationship, although unions may seek to apply their own selection criteria and to influence the outcome. Access to individual employees allows management to put the case for redundancy more clearly and specifically. This can be done in terms of justification for the redundancies themselves (for example, the firm is not competitive because it is overstaffed) and in terms of the financial position of the individual employee. Employees may well accept the economic logic of the management's position and/or recognize the management's determination and ability to achieve the redundancies.

A third way in which managerial control may be enhanced by VR is through the effect on the total number of redundancies. In the case of a positive response to VR, management may be able to increase the number of redundancies above that originally planned. For example, under British Telecom's Release 92 Scheme the target number of redundancies was 20,000, but because of the good response the company increased the figure to 29,000 (that is, by 45 per cent). Thus VR may allow management to increase the number of redundancies while at the same time reducing the scope for opposition.

Finally, management may be able to implement redundancies more quickly under VR than they would if they had to negotiate compulsory redundancies with a union and/or consult individually with those to be made compulsorily redundant. The timing can be controlled by incentives and penalties (see below, pp. 30–1).

Since large redundancies may occur in waves, the effect of VR may be to weaken the union's position in trying to oppose future redundancies. It may affect even the terms on which future redundancies are available, for example, the level of the payment itself. A queue of volunteers may be seen as indicating a plentiful supply from sellers of jobs. An employer (the monopoly buyer) may feel this is an indicator that no further price increase is necessary, that is, that the level of RP is adequate for the company's purpose. Part of the union's weak position may stem from the loss of experienced officials in an earlier wave of redundancies, leaving younger, less experienced people to take their positions.

## *Organizational change*

The potential for redundancy to be associated with the restructuring of work and gains in productivity is discussed in chapter 3. The point here is that VR may assist in changing the character of the whole organization. The organization may be revitalized because VR tends to encourage a disproportionate number of volunteers from the upper end of the organization's age structure. The reasons for this are the availability of an early and enhanced company pension, and redundancy payments which increase with age and length of employment. Voluntary redundancy therefore presents an opportunity to revitalize the organization by reducing the average age of its workforce and opening up promotion possibilities.

However, while inefficient parts of the organization may be removed and the least productive workers may leave, this will not *necessarily* be the case. For example, the best talent could go, leaving the least able, since the former may have opportunities elsewhere and the latter not. Moreover, while promotion opportunities are opened up initially, they may be closed later because those promoted have a long tenure of office. This may result in frustration and loss of morale because of diminished prospects, and a lack of dynamism because of the absence of changes in personnel.

Voluntary redundancy can be a good technique for revitalizing an organization if management can control and direct its use. This involves determining the individuals and organizational parts to be removed. Both management and union will need to consider, and, if possible influence, the shape of what is left after the redundancy volunteers have gone. Both have an interest in securing a proper distribution of jobs, skills, age and experience. Since one effect of VR is to give more influence to the individual employee, it might be argued that union and management have a common interest in human resource planning, retraining and safety to counter the effects of what might be, in part, an unpredictable pattern of individual departures. Both may wish to aim VR schemes at particular (although not necessarily the same) sections of the workforce.

Management may be able to use a VR exercise to alter the conduct of industrial relations. While collective bargaining with a union may continue, management may be able to use the exercise as a vehicle for increasing control over important areas such as staffing, work practices, pay and productivity. It cannot be said that VR inevitably works in these ways but a valid conclusion is that VR can be associated with redefined power relations and dramatic industrial relations changes.

## Conditions Favouring the Effective Use of VR

The fact that management want (or are willing) to use VR is a prerequisite for the introduction of the technique, but certain conditions encourage, or perhaps are necessary for, its effective deployment. These were referred to earlier as facilitating factors, to be distinguished from the factors which cause the VR technique to be adopted in the first place (see above, p. 19 ff). The facilitating factors comprise:

- availability of sufficient finance;
- favourable workforce characteristics;
- absence of union opposition or control; and
- availability of work for non-volunteers.

### *Availability of sufficient finance*

It seems clear that more money will be needed if an individual is to be persuaded rather than forced to leave. (British Telecom's Release 92 Scheme is reported as costing over £1 billion: 29,000 redundancies in a workforce of 200,000.) As noted above (p. 18), the essence of the VR bargain is the employer's offer to dismiss with a RP in exchange for acceptance of dismissal by the employee. This exchange takes place in a context where, providing the employee qualifies, he or she will receive a minimum level of payment laid down by law (see chapter 9). A key factor in VR, therefore, is likely to be the availability of RPs in excess of this statutory minimum. Another important factor will be the facility for early retirement with enhanced pensionable service. It seems possible that trades unionism is not only likely to encourage management to think in terms of VR, but also may induce circumstances which will make it easier to adopt VR. Extra-statutory RPs, good pension arrangements and higher pay for those with longer service are three examples.

Any financial help from outside the company will increase the chances of using VR successfully. Until 1986 all employers in Great Britain had a rebate from the State Redundancy Fund to offset part of the costs of redundancy.[2] Thereafter, until 1990, when it was abolished altogether, the rebate was given only to small firms.[3] In the coal, steel and shipbuilding industries European Community money has been used to improve the redundancy package, and VR has been used widely in all three cases.[4] The ICI scheme has been even more generous, but in this case the company's own profits were sufficient to allow it to make an attractive offer.

## Workforce characteristics

Age-structures, length of employment patterns and earnings levels may be relevant to the effective use of VR. An age-structure with a high proportion of people in the early retirement age-category means that what is typically the best financial deal is available to a relatively large proportion of the workforce. (Of course, an employer may prefer to control the financial and other aspects of VR in a different way, for example, so as to preserve experience and minimize the proportion of older people made redundant.) A relatively old, stable workforce, with substantial length of employment in individual cases, will increase the size of RPs because the statutory formula is based partly upon age and length of employment. The same applies to level of earnings, subject to the computation rules described in chapter 9. Where the extra-statutory payments adopt the statutory criteria, viz. age, length of employment and pay, the effect on the size of RPs will be magnified further.

Research in the United States suggests that trades unionism is associated with more stable workforces.[5] If this were true generally in Great Britain it would be expected, all other things being equal, that unionized workplaces would have age-structures more suited to VR than would non-unionized workplaces.

## Absence of union opposition or control

Next there is the question of union attitude towards VR and the extent to which a union can prevent its members volunteering if it thinks it is necessary to do so. Clearly the latter will be of relevance only in the case of union opposition to VR. In such circumstances an employer may be tempted to communicate directly with employees in the hope of bringing forth volunteers. If the union has little control over its members this may prove successful. In highly-disciplined areas, however, (for example, parts of the printing industry) this may simply worsen the industrial relations climate without achieving the desired end.

Of course it should not be forgotten that the initiative for VR may come from the union rather than the employer.[6] The motive may be realistic and/or democratic. The *realistic* motive starts from the view that job losses are inevitable, and concentrates upon the avoidance of compulsory redundancies. The aim is to protect everyone who is a member by negotiating job security for some and compensation for the others. In contrast, the *democratic* motive attaches primacy to the wishes of the members in the place where the redundancies have been declared. Whereas the realistic motive relates (at least in part) to the union's strength *vis-à-vis* the employer the democratic motive is determined by the union's relations with its members.

## Availability of work for stayers

VR assumes that work is available, at least in the medium term, for those who want to stay. In cases of closure, therefore, workers who do not volunteer will need to have the opportunity to transfer to another site. More usually VR will be applicable to company slimming exercises rather than to closures, that is, where the size of the workforce of a continuing operation is diminished in order to increase productivity and reduce unit costs.

The operation of the above factors is likely to help make VR effective in practice. In addition, employers may be able to influence the supply of volunteers in ways indicated later (see pp. 34–6). Voluntary redundancy may be particularly (but not universally or exclusively) suited for use in relatively large organizations. A larger firm first of all may be better placed to pay for an attractive redundancy package. Included in this would be the greater likelihood of an occupational pension scheme being in operation, and its availability as part of the package. Another dimension is the greater likelihood of suitable alternative work being available in a larger firm. Clearly VR is easier to achieve when an alternative job is available if a person's existing job becomes unnecessary, although if the alternative is attractive this might reduce the take-up of VR.

## Avoiding the Drawbacks

### Selection

Where unions and management exert little control over VR, the employee's influence will be enhanced and VR may become a form of self-selection for redundancy. The volunteer population may become an irresistible force and the pattern of volunteers may largely determine the distribution of actual redundancies. In such a case, the redundancies may occur disproportionately among older and more experienced employees who are eligible for an early and enhanced pension. More generally, the pattern of redundancies may lack production rationale and may result in a range of post-redundancy problems (see chapter 3).[7] Such lack of control by management is not an inevitable feature of voluntary redundancy. Much will depend upon the financial and trading position of the company. If a massive short-term crisis means that the company needs to achieve large savings quickly, VR is likely to have a relatively free rein. Where a company is less pressured, policy-making can be more considered and a less short-term view taken. Under such circumstances there is no reason why management cannot effectively control the VR process.[8] Indeed, some measure of control may be possible even in extreme circumstances.

The first stage in controlling selection of those to be made redundant under VR is to determine who is to be allowed to volunteer. Management may wish to exclude certain categories of staff from the VR scheme and/or may wish to target the scheme at others. For example, staff with key skills and experience may be excluded, that is, not given the chance to volunteer, while staff with poor health or disciplinary records may be specifically invited to volunteer. Where there is work restructuring or a partial closure of plant, some staff may be pushed into volunteering by the disappearance of their jobs.

Having established the coverage of the VR scheme (and any emphasis within that coverage), management will need to determine criteria for selecting from the pool of volunteers. In applying the criteria, management will want to retain a right of veto in any particular, individual case. This is the second stage in the process of controlling selection. If management wish to preserve skills and experience they may apply the LIFO principle, although they will invariably wish to temper it with managerial interest criteria. Unions may put forward their own criteria. In practice, redundancy volunteers are often selected on the basis of what might be termed the first in, first out (or seniority) principle; the longest serving go first because they have the best financial deal and are keenest to go. For different reasons, this criterion is often popular with both management and unions. Other criteria which have been used include: poor health or disciplinary record, lack of promotion prospects and date of volunteering (that is, first come, first served). Where management have preserved skills, experience etc. by excluding staff from the VR scheme, the criteria for selection from the pool of volunteers may be of less importance (although the criteria should not be such as to leave management open to successful unfair dismissal claims – see chapter 7). Where the supply of volunteers does not reach the redundancy target, management may wish to consider ways in which the supply could be increased.

Human resource planning will be necessary to determine the post-redundancy shape of the organization in terms of occupations, work locations, skills, experience and so on. This will dictate the criteria

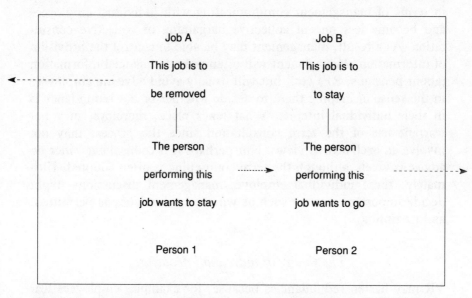

**Figure 2** Matching the retained workforce and the jobs available in the context of a voluntary redundancy scheme
Matching involves
(a) removal of job A
(b) redundancy of person 2
(c) retention of job B
(d) person 1 performing job B

used in respect of the coverage of the VR scheme and any selection from the pool of volunteers. Some mechanism will then be needed to match the retained labour force to the jobs available. Figure 2 shows the position diagrammatically.

The vacancies created by the acceptance of volunteers are matched with the workers whose jobs have disappeared but who wish to remain with the company. Local operational management may try to dissuade volunteers in their area unless they feel that they will get adequate replacements.

## The supply of information

VR is likely to require a greater information base than is necessary in a compulsory redundancy. This flows from the fact that under VR the individual has to make a choice. In order to decide what is in his or her own best interest that individual will need information. Under VR, consultation may be more individually-based than under compulsory redundancy in a unionized setting. The process may develop in terms of management communicating with individual employees and become less one of collective bargaining or collective consultation. As a result, management may be able to control the provision of information. Management will often provide financial information (about pensions, RPs etc.) but will usually avoid advising employees in the sense of helping them to decide whether or not redundancy is in their individual interest. What takes place, therefore, may not warrant use of the term consultation since the process may not involve an exchange of views. Nor perhaps is it counselling, since no advice is given, although the term counselling is often adopted. Ultimately, these individual employee/management discussions might decide important matters such as whether redundancy is permitted, and its timing.

## The timing of individual departures

VR may hasten redundancies because, for example, employees fear that the financial package may be on offer for only a limited period, or believe that an insufficient take-up of VR will bring about compulsory redundancies. Various devices may be used to influence the timing of redundancies. First, part of the VR bargain can be that the date of dismissal will be at management's discretion, albeit within a reasonable time period (for example, six months). Second, some or all of the extra-statutory RP can be reduced for dismissals occurring after a certain date, so encouraging early volunteering. An example of such a formula is given below.

$$\text{Extra-statutory RP} = 13 \text{ weeks' pay} \times \frac{a}{b}$$

where: a is the number of complete weeks between termination and 31 March 1993, with a maximum set at 25

and: b is the number of complete weeks between 1 October 1992 and 31 March 1993.

Since b is a period of 25 weeks each complete week of employment after the cut-off date of 1 October would mean a $\frac{1}{25}$ or 4 per cent reduction in the size of the extra-statutory RP. The formula can be adjusted to make it more or less punitive. More positively, the RP package can be improved for those who volunteer early (for example, through enhanced holiday pay entitlement). In the British Telecom case, those who left by 31 July 1992 received a bonus equal to 25 per cent of their salary. The response was overwhelming and management later saw the bonus as being too generous. Retention payments can be made to those willing to defer their departure in order to assist in any rundown of plant.[9]

Management will need to decide whether the VR scheme is to be used for a fixed period or allowed to continue indefinitely. The former might apply where VR was designed to allow a once-for-all response to a current and specific need for reduced staffing. The latter might be the case where there was a continuing need to present a favourable early-retirement package in order to reduce the size and average age of the workforce over a longer period of time. Even in the former case, management may wish to spread the redundancies to some extent in order to avoid the operational dislocation caused by a large number of people leaving together. Also, such a policy would take some of the strain off the administration, which can become overwhelmed if there is a flood of voluntary redundancy applications which need to be processed within a very short period.

## The level of finance

Judging the correct level of RPs may be difficult. Under-finance may result in the company's problem not being solved and in recourse to compulsory redundancy, although schemes can be adjusted if time permits. But over-finance also has its problems. Not only is it a misallocation of resources, but it is likely to create a morale problem. A response which is much too large inevitably results in reduced morale among those who wish to leave but are being prevented from doing so. This is reported as having happened at British Telecom in 1992, and apparently management had to take steps to counteract it: they organized courses to help maintain morale.

### The use of a company framework policy

A multi-level approach is possible, with the decision to use VR made at corporate level, the job loss targets decided at works level and selection and manning adjustments determined at departmental level. A difference may be perceived between a closure, the decision on which can be handed down from above, and a slim-down, where local negotiation is required on such matters as flexibility. An advantage of determining the scale of redundancies at a high level, after local consultations, is that control can be secured and local vested interests overcome.

## Factors Influencing the Supply of Volunteers

The supply of volunteers in a redundancy situation is governed by management and trades union factors and by individual employee choice. The management and union factors, influenced by relative bargaining power, can be seen as determining whether a particular individual has a choice, and the manner and timing of the expression of that choice. The individual then makes a decision – whether or not to volunteer – taking into account one or more of a number of influences relating to his or her own welfare. The various management and union factors may be seen as determining the framework within which the individual exercises his or her freedom of choice. The individual choice characteristics – a mix of work and personal factors – then operate to determine the supply of volunteers. All of this is shown diagrammatically in figure 3. Left out of the reckoning are macroeconomic conditions, since in any particular case these are constant. They comprise factors which clearly could affect the number of volunteers in redundancies, but cannot be adjusted by management or unions in the short term although in the long term they might be able to achieve change via the political process. Such factors include statutory financial help with RPs, statutory

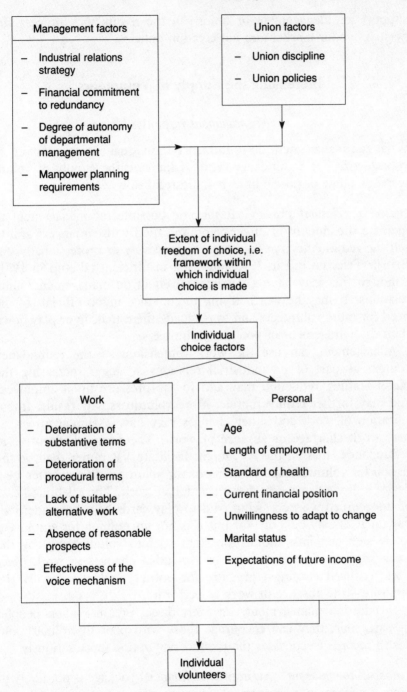

**Figure 3**  Factors determining the supply of volunteers

support for management or unions in the redundancy process and positive labour market and job creation policies.

## Increasing the Supply of Volunteers

### *Management responses*

What can management do to influence individual choice in favour of volunteering for redundancy, and so increase the supply of volunteers? A range of possibilities is indicated below.

*Industrial relations strategy*   It may be possible for management to increase the amount of direct communication with employees and to sell the redundancy package more aggressively or professionally, (as British Telecom did in 1992 following insufficient take-up in 1991) although this may have a detrimental effect on management/union relations. It may be worth trying to convince union officials of the need for more volunteers and to persuade them to drop or play down their discouragement of potential volunteers.

Management can use the work dimensions of the redundancy context as part of its industrial relations strategy. Increasing the target staffing reduction may add to the pressure upon employees and may further reduce morale. More volunteers may result. Intensification of work and other changes may have a similar effect, as may work shortage or absence of work. The financial incentive in redundancy, that is, the RP, might facilitate VR rather than be the reason for volunteering. The reasons for volunteering may often be a desire to leave because of dissatisfaction at work. The celebrated case of unoccupied workers being paid to play cards or watch videos all day (at ICI) may be a one-off but it is not uncommon for employees to be sickened into submission (that is, into volunteering) by the work context. Sometimes this has included changes in work practices, reduced earnings, pressure for output, and occasionally the opposite – the absence of work to perform.

In addition management can exert direct pressure upon people. In particular, they can encourage those with poor disciplinary and health records to consider the redundancy option more seriously.

*Financial commitment*   An improved financial package is not likely to cause tensions in management-union relations, but it may be an expensive way of increasing the supply of volunteers. If the RP is increased, a higher proportion of those taking a cost/benefit approach to VR will find that expected benefits exceed expected costs (other things being equal). The RP may be seen as the cost to an employer of persuading the marginal volunteer. The effect of increasing the level of RP will be weaker if the view that the money is a facilitator rather than a motivator is correct. Moreover, increases in the level of RP may be subject to the law of diminishing marginal utility as far as the employees are concerned. If this were the case, the higher the level of RP the greater the marginal increase in RP which would be needed to achieve a specified increase in the supply of volunteers.

The pay system itself may be used to encourage volunteering. A bonus scheme based on the value added principle and taking into account labour costs may provide the vehicle for this. Potential volunteers as well as stayers would be able to see a connection between the supply of volunteers and the security of those who remain. Any stigma attached to volunteering – selling jobs – might give way to a more positive view. A direct linkage between pay and job losses makes the point even more explicitly, for example, a 3 per cent bonus if staffing is reduced to 10,000, 4 per cent if reduced to 9,750 etc.

*Other aspects of policy*   Senior management could take a tougher line with departmental managers who were discouraging volunteers in order to minimize destaffing in their own areas. The number of redundancies required can be handed down from corporate to departmental level, with instructions that dilution must not take place. Again, management can sacrifice some of its human resource planning objectives for the immediate cause of increasing the supply of volunteers, meeting the redundancy target and effecting the necessary savings. It can restrict the use of veto over individuals, and open the VR process to all employees if not already the case.

*Individual choice*   It has been noted that the work aspects of the redundancy context can be manipulated to provide a tool for shaping the supply of volunteers. In as much as the union's voice can be ignored employees will be encouraged to use the exit solution, subject to consideration of labour market conditions if the intention is to remain in the labour market. However, there may be a price to pay in terms of employee morale. Those who do not volunteer may be further alienated and may respond through increased absence, lower productivity etc., thus imposing costs on the company.

As far as the personal factors are concerned, there is perhaps less scope for management initiative. However, there are *some* possibilities. Probably the most expensive of these would be to reduce the age at which an early pension was payable. Since such arrangements are effective only if the actual number of pensionable years is enhanced, this is bound to involve substantial costs. Other possibilities would be to improve the financial package for certain groups, such as those suffering from ill health, or to restrict the volunteer's losses, for example, by better or more counselling and assistance with job search or retraining.

*Demand side changes*   Another type of management response to a shortfall in the number of volunteers is to reduce demand. Employers can take the supply as fixed (by the actual response) and choose from the following options, viz:

- meet the shortfall through compulsory redundancy;
- look for other savings instead (for example, through improved work practices);
- reduce the total savings sought in the particular time period.

Indeed, a response comprising all three of the above is possible, although clearly avoidance of compulsory redundancy will be desirable if constructive management-union relationships are to be maintained, employee morale kept up and public image protected (because, for example, it might have implications for sales or recruitment).

## Union responses

There may be circumstances in which a union would want to increase the supply of volunteers. This could be the case, for instance, if management indicates that a shortfall will be met by compulsory redundancies. In such a situation a union can be seen as having three main lines of approach. First, it can put a more favourable case to the members and try to elicit a better response. Second, it may attempt to persuade the employer to improve part or all of the redundancy package. Finally, it may relax any controls that it has exerted over members' freedom to volunteer or depart. A union may prefer to try to persuade the employer to reduce the staff reduction target (and achieve savings in other ways).

It is clear that VR can be an effective means of dealing with redundancy if the financial and other conditions are appropriate. It is also clear that redundancy may provide an opportunity for organizational change. The next chapter explores how redundancy may be used as a vehicle for such change.

## Notes

1 The principle that agreement to redundancy does not prevent there being a dismissal was established in *Burton, Allton and Johnson Ltd.* v. *Peck* and endorsed in *Morley and ors* v. *C.T. Morley Ltd.* The principle holds regardless of whether the employee is asked to volunteer for redundancy or takes the initiative and applies for it. In either case the employee is volunteering for dismissal. However, there must be a dismissal if there is to be a redundancy. If the employee resigns prior to notice of dismissal, there will have been no dismissal even if the employee definitely would have been dismissed (*Morton Sundour Fabrics Ltd.* v. *Shaw*). Voluntary redundancy can be distinguished from early retirement, which is normally mutual termination (although this would have to be decided on the facts). In *Birch and Humber* v. *The University of Liverpool*, the employer made clear that it was not a redundancy scheme and that termination required mutual agreement.

2 The Wages Act 1986 restricted the rebate – which by that time had been reduced to 35 per cent – to employers with fewer than ten employees (s. 27).

3 The Employment Act 1989 abolished the rebate altogether with effect from 1990. It remains to be seen whether this will make VR less attractive to employers since VR lays more emphasis on the redundancy of older workers who have larger RPs.

4 See, for example, the European Communities (Iron and Steel Employees Re-adaptation Benefits Scheme) Regulations, SI 1974/908 and SI 1979/954, as amended.

5 Freeman, R.B. and Medoff, J.L., *What do Trades Unions do?* New York: Basic Books Inc., 1984, p. 109.

6 This was the case, for example, in the Bristol engineering industry in the early 1970s. Dey, I.F., *A study of the formulation and implementation of policies relating to redundancy and unemployment by the AUEW District Committee, Bristol, 1970–72*, Ph.D. thesis, University of Bristol, 1979. Some unions may prefer RPs to lay-offs or wage reductions.

7 For example, the operation of the voluntary redundancy schemes for university staffs in the early 1980s resulted in age and occupational imbalance among the remaining staff. Too many people aged over 55

were allowed to leave, causing a bulge in the 40–55 age group, and there was a greater than average reduction in numbers in engineering, technology, maths and computer science, areas which were supposed to be protected. The Public Accounts Committee thought that applications were pushed through with too much haste and too little care. (Public Accounts Committee, *Report of an Inquiry into Redundancy Schemes for University Staffs*, London: HMSO, 1986.)

8  A good example of such control is the British Telecom scheme, completed in 1991, under which it was planned to reduce the number of managers from 43,000 to 37,000. The scheme had two stages. First, volunteers were targeted and invited to volunteer. Second, management jobs were redefined or eliminated and managers applied for the available jobs. Those not appointed used a clearing house for vacancies elsewhere in the company. If that failed, there was either voluntary redundancy or early retirement. Apparently, there were no enforced redundancies (*Financial Times*, 10 June 1991).

9  The alternative approach is to reduce RPs for those who will not stay. The US computer manufacturer Unisys had plans to halve RPs for employees who left before the closure of its Livingston plant (*Financial Times*, 22 October 1991).

# 3
# Business Performance and Redundancy

Redundancy may be a problem, with potential for legal and industrial challenges, disruption and cost, but it also provides an opportunity for increased productivity. This chapter considers the means by which productivity can be increased in the context of redundancy, but also deals with the operational difficulties which can occur in the post-redundancy period. Finally, an attempt is made to analyse redundancy in terms of its principal costs and benefits.

## Redundancy as a Means of Improving Productivity

### Redundancy as an opportunity for increasing productivity

Any trades union is likely to be in a weak bargaining position and some employees, subject to the financial deal on offer, will want to leave. Also, among those who remain there is likely to be a recognition that changes are necessary. The potential for reduced staffing in continuing operations, with greater efficiency, and unnecessary functions removed, may be immense. Clearly, organizations may increase productivity by closing unproductive plants. The focus here, however, is upon what has come to be known as slimming – reduced staffing in continuing operations – the paradigm case of the last decade.

Redundancy, therefore, is a situation in which long-standing problems may be successfully tackled. These include not only the obvious areas of overstaffing and lack of flexibility, but also unproductive and unnecessary overtime, excessive absence, poor discipline and overgrown or superfluous functions. Redundancy is a time when new standards can be laid down as the organization gears up to operating in a changed environment.

## Means of effecting redundancies

Experience in recent years suggests a range of devices which may be used in order to achieve productivity increases through redundancy while the operation of the organization continues. Often, these devices have been used in concert. An example, taken from the manufacturing sector, is given in table 1 to indicate the means available and to illustrate how they might be used.

**Table 1** Achieving productivity increases through redundancy – an example from manufacturing industry

|  | No. of redundancies |
| --- | --- |
| Increased flexibility | 353 |
| Use of contractors | 309 |
| Reduced activity or services | 257 |
| Reorganization | 203 |
| Work restructuring | 127 |
| Increased workload | 111 |
| Increased use of equipment | 52 |
| Total | 1,412 |

Table 1 underestimates the importance of increased flexibility and the use of contractors, since these are sometimes a feature of reduced activity and reorganization. Since flexibility and restructuring both involve job redesign, it is clear that this can be a major influence. Perhaps the most significant aspect of the picture presented in Table 1, however, is the totality of approach; a wide range of methods can be used.

## Labour flexibility

*Types of flexibility* The ACAS survey in 1987 used the term employment flexibility to cover four main approaches to change.[1] Numerical flexibility relates to the size of the workforce and allows organizations to respond to seasonal and other changes in demand for their services and products. The principal means of effecting control over workforce size are adjustments to the scale of employment of part-timers, temporary workers and subcontractors. Functional flexibility refers to the blurring of demarcation lines between different categories of employee. It is particularly relevant between crafts,[2] and between craftsmen and production workers, but also may occur between blue and white collar workers. A third form of flexibility is in respect of hours of work. The aims of flexibility here have been to maximise the use of expensive equipment and to match production or services more closely to customer needs. An increase in shift working and more flexible shift patterns are the usual result. Finally, there is flexibility of labour costs and, conversely, rewards. The primary device here is some sort of linkage between rewards and performance in order to contribute more directly to organizational goals and to allow for labour cost reduction where performance is reduced. The pay-performance link is discussed further in chapter 4.

*Implications of flexibility*   ACAS has found that flexibility is generally increasing and encourages management to be aware of its implications.[3] The increasing tendency to link pay with performance involves the development of plant level bargaining; pay structures are based on rewards for flexibility and the acquisition and practice of necessary skills rather than upon the idea of a rate for the job. On a group basis, such pay systems may be rooted in the concept of added value (see chapter 4).

Flexibility can lead to higher labour turnover and absenteeism, and a lack of commitment. These characteristics are sometimes associated with part-time and temporary employment and the use of contractors. To offset such tendencies, employers may need to be more careful in their recruitment and selection processes. They may need to achieve more effective induction, and better communication generally, in order to create a stronger sense of organizational identification and commitment on the part of the worker.

The need for increased training is one of the more obvious implications of flexibility. Where employees perform a wider range of tasks, the need is clear, but supervisors too will have wider demands placed upon them, and they also will require training. They will need to enhance their communication skills and training may be necessary to achieve this. Finally, functional flexibility may lead to new management and supervisory structures. In particular, the notion of people working in teams is increasingly popular, and in such systems there is a tendency to have a team leader, to dispense with the position of supervisor and to have a generally flatter management structure.[4]

*The flexible firm*   Organizations may be flexible in some or all of the ways described earlier. The concept of a flexible firm, however, seems to be rooted particularly in the idea that speedy adjustments can be made to the size of the labour force. The means of achieving such adjustments are the recruitment or dismissal of part-time and temporary workers and contractors. These, including perhaps some home-workers, might be seen as a peripheral workforce with limited rights and security, to be contrasted with the core employees who are permanent and enjoy pensions and other rights.

Regardless of how far this model is grounded in reality, it is clear that there is much use of peripheral workers and the warning from ACAS about the need to integrate such workers is of considerable importance. ACAS also stresses the need for a participative style of management if the benefits of the various forms of flexibility are to be fully realized. In short, flexibility seems to warrant a human resource management approach, based on maximum use of the organization's human potential, and integration of the individual on the basis of commitment rather than control.

## Other means of change

*Use of contractors*   One of the most common ways in which redundancies have been effected is by transferring work to contractors. This has been particularly true in respect of service functions; for example, in table 1, the use of contractors for catering services accounted for 124 of the 309 redundancies effected by this means. However, the scope for use of contractors is much wider than this and in a manufacturing context might include:

- emergencies;
- occasions when plant is stopped by mechanical failure or extended repairs;
- situations where the demands upon in-house maintenance staff are particularly great;
- occasions where there is need for skilled specialists;
- the construction and installation of new plant;
- situations where there is a danger of not being able to fulfil contractual obligations e.g. where warranty, guarantee or penalty clauses operate;
- work to be done off-site; and
- the replacement or supplementing of production ancillary workers or even production workers themselves.

*Reduced activity or services*  This category includes production cut-backs, reductions in service departments and reductions in shifts. An example of the last-mentioned might be a move from 21-shift, 4-crew working to a 15-shift, 3-crew system. An example of a cutback in services is a reduction in a work study department. The moves in recent years towards pay-performance links have meant that the need for work measurement has declined.

Sometimes, reductions in activity have been accompanied by increased flexibility. A smaller staff carrying out the same range of duties, albeit on a smaller scale, has meant that a wider range of tasks has to be performed by each employee. Similarly, cutbacks have often been accompanied by the use of contractors to carry out some of the work formerly done by employees. Any reduction in activity has also been an opportunity to look at whether economies can be achieved through increased use of equipment.

*Reorganization*  Reorganization involves a degree of institutional change. One aspect of this in large firms in the manufacturing sector has been the centralization of maintenance and production services previously provided by service workers being attached to particular operational departments. This implies a degree of skill flexibility (or at least the use of existing skills in a variety of contexts) and mobility within the site. Sometimes, reorganization has involved the use of contractors.

*Work restructuring*  Whereas flexibility involves taking on extra and/or different tasks (and in some cases adopting more flexible attitudes towards hours and location of work) restructuring is taken to mean the substantial redesign of whole jobs. Clearly the dividing line is difficult to draw in practice even though there is a qualitative difference between the two in theory.

*Increased workload*  Typically this means no change in the nature of duties, but rather an increase in the amount of work done per person. This has been a dominant feature in staff areas in manufacturing, for example, finance, planning and wages departments and in the service sector more generally. This may be contrasted with flexibility, which implies a change in duties, and which has often been a feature in production areas.

*Increased use of equipment* Usually this has been new equipment, often computerized, which has replaced manual or mechanical systems.

## Implementing change

In implementing changes designed to increase productivity, management will need to bear in mind the various legal constraints. While the law allows dismissal for redundancy (subject to the fairness of the manner in which the redundancy has been handled – see chapter 7), it does not generally permit an employer to make unilateral changes to employees' terms of employment. Some aspects of employment may not be contractual terms, for example, conditions of employment which management legitimately may alter, or discretionary matters such as a benefit provided by management on a goodwill basis. Other changes may be permitted if the contract terms have been drawn widely enough, for example, to allow movement between sites.

If none of these apply it will be necessary to secure employee consent by express individual agreement, agreement in practice (that is by the employee working under the new term) or through an agreement with a trades union (providing the term becomes incorporated into the individual employee's contract of employment). Where there is no consent, unilateral change leaves the way open for management to be sued in respect of breach of contract. Dismissal for refusal to agree to reasonable change, possibly with the offer of a new contract on different terms, removes the threat of action for remedies for breach of contract as long as the dismissal is in accordance with the terms of the contract, for example, by providing due notice. However, such a dismissal may still need defending as fair if an employee pursues a claim to an industrial tribunal.

## Post-Redundancy Adjustment

### Voluntary redundancy

As noted in chapter 2, voluntary redundancy may solve a company's immediate crisis but it may cause particular post-redundancy problems if it is not fully controlled. The pattern of volunteers may influence the pattern of actual redundancies if the company's general policy has been to allow volunteers to go. Even where there are attempts to control the resultant occupational structure, the post-redundancy workforce may not be exactly what the production process requires. In short, voluntary redundancy may make effective human resource planning difficult.

The retained workforce may be young and may have some deficiencies in terms of skills, training and experience.[5] There may be imbalances between and within departments, as well as areas of work where destaffing simply has gone too far. A good example of the latter effect is where destaffing occurs directly as a result of the non-replacement of a redundancy volunteer. Some departmental managers may discourage volunteers within their department if they anticipate that there might be non-replacement. Attempts at blocking, however, are fraught with difficulties because of the inevitable resentment which results and the consequent negative effect on work peroformance.[6]

The above effects need to be kept in perspective. Post-redundancy staffing problems caused by having less than full control over VR can be tackled once the survival of the company is assured. They are relatively minor problems and in any case persist only in the short term. Nevertheless, solutions have to be found. How can lack of training, skills and experience, and in some cases insufficient staffing, affect a company and how can that company respond?

The principal effects may be losses of production caused by bottlenecks, an increase in lost-time injuries and the slower through-put achieved by less experienced and younger staff. The quality of output may also suffer and there may be an increased incidence of damage to hardware and scrapping of materials. Because voluntary redundancy typically is most attractive to older employees, many experienced staff are likely to have been among the volunteers. Thus, relatively young people may be stepping into senior jobs for which they are not equipped at that time.

All of the above result in costs for a company as do the remedies which are required. A substantial training initiative may be needed, with a particular emphasis upon direct job knowledge and skills, and safety requirements. In certain work areas there may need to be some recruitment. More generally, like natural wastage, voluntary redundancy does not necessarily slim down the inefficient parts of the organization. Further, the leavers may have included some of the most talented young people who might have contributed most to the future of the organization.

What can be said, therefore, about the effect of VR on the longer-term character of a company? As noted, one of the major effects may be to reduce substantially the average age of the workforce. While lack of experience may be the negative implication of this, the positive side may be the introduction of greater drive and flexibility of attitude (for example, towards change). Among other things, this may assist an organization in the introduction of new technology. A second possible effect is the removal of employees who are disaffected, those suffering ill-health and those who have a poor work record (for instance, bad timekeeping). Those in the second and third of the above categories (and those in the first, if known) can be encouraged to volunteer. A third possible effect is undoubtedly the loss of some young talent. A lack of opportunity (and in the case of certain employees the existence of transferable skills) may be the underlying cause. A fourth effect is that some of the least employable stay because of a lack of opportunities elsewhere.

Finally, there may be a significant industrial relations effect. Trades union officials may have been prominent among the redundancy volunteers. In some cases it has been known for the union to lose a whole generation of its officials during a voluntary redundancy exercise, compared with the normal trickle of officials retiring from their positions or failing to be re-elected. This situation may be to management's advantage but it could also create difficulties. New and younger officials may be unfamiliar with established procedures and terms, and be less effective as communicators because of a lack of experience and training. There may be few experienced officials left to assist them.

### Flexible working

The introduction of flexible working is likely to require employees to perform a wider range of tasks, possibly in an increased number of contexts. There may be a need for job and safety training. Since management may also have a wider remit, the training need is likely to extend to them. Management may need to operate new systems, for example, where there has been a reorganization such as that involving a centralization of services. The same will be true where contractors have replaced direct employees. In addition, there may be new systems of payment involving links between pay and performance, and new structures, such as those based on team working. An increased workload and more demanding work may be a source of stress; investment in stress counselling and time-management may be a cost that has to be offset against the productivity gains flowing from redundancy.

## *Types of problem*

As a result of the above analysis it is possible to pinpoint a number of different types of human resource management problem which may occur in the post-redundancy period:

- skill and experience deficiencies;
- staff shortages;
- difficulties in effectively implementing flexibility;
- problems arising out of relations with trades unions;
- low morale among staff.

It has been noted that skill and experience deficiencies may give rise to problems in respect of the quantity and quality of output and in relation to safety, and may lead to damage being caused. There is likely to be a training requirement, and where safety is a factor, that requirement may be founded in law. Staff shortages may require post-redundancy recruitment. The problems arising from the introduction of flexibility are likely to require training, and the operation of new systems and stuctures. Union problems may stem from having a cadre of inexperienced union officials. Where the union has resisted redundancy, it may be less co-operative in the post-redundancy period.

A major concern will be how to increase morale among staff who have just experienced a generally negative and insecure period within their organization. Some of those remaining may have been prevented from volunteering for redundancy, or refused redundancy after volunteering. A related problem, where flexibility has been increased post-redundancy through the use of more part-time and temporary staff, is how to integrate such employees into the organization and achieve commitment on their part. Training, communication, rewards and all the other factors that bear on motivation are likely to have a high profile in the post-redundancy period. This will be so particularly in a context of increased production pressure and the performance by employees of more varied tasks. Increased earnings and improved security of employment may be financed out of some of the savings from redundancy, and can be seen as a cost of the redundancy. Where many older employees have left (for example, under voluntary redundancy), the existence of promotion opportunities may be of considerable assistance to management in creating an atmosphere of revival and optimism.

## The Costs and Benefits of Redundancy

### *Redundancy as an investment*

Redundancy is a response to a problem – a change in the conditions facing an organization – but it also presents an opportunity for change. Costs are involved, and these may be greater where employees are to be persuaded rather than forced to leave, but there are also benefits because redundancy can be used as a vehicle for improving productivity.[7] Thus redundancy assumes the character of an investment and there seems to be no reason why the accounting aspects of the redundancy decision should not be treated in the same way as any other investment. Of course if redundancy is inevitable an investment *has* to be made, but there may still be a choice of strategy involving the investment of differing amounts (for example, a minimum investment in compulsory redundancy as opposed to a larger investment in VR). Organizations may adopt differing accounting practices for investment appraisal; here the aim is to do no more than identify the principal heads of cost and benefit, recognizing in the process that some of them may be quantifiable only in an arbitrary, rough and ready sort of way.

### *The costs of redundancy*

The costs of redundancy may be substantial especially if it is proposed to rely on VR. For example, but perhaps *in extremis*, British Telecom is reported as spending over £1 billion on its Release 92 programme, which involved 29,000 redundancies. Some £390 million was set aside for 18,500 redundancies in 1991. More generally, the costs of redundancy can be divided between immediate one-offs, short-term costs and longer-term costs.

*One-off costs*   These are the redundancy payments themselves (and associated costs such as pay in lieu of notice) and the value of payments into the pension fund to finance the enhancement of pensionable service. Together, these are likely to account for a very large proportion of the total costs involved, and are likely to be identified in the company's annual accounts.

*Short-term costs* Where compulsory redundancy is used these may include:

- union disruption to operations and lack of co-operation in the post-redundancy period; and
- damage to the company's image resulting in difficulty in recruiting suitable staff, loss of staff commitment and perhaps reduced sales.

Where VR is used there may be:

- skill and experience deficiencies which result in production losses, training costs and accident costs; and
- staff shortages with attendant production losses and subsequent recruitment costs.

The introduction of flexible working may be associated with production costs, training costs and the cost of introducing new systems and structures. Also, in the short term, there is the loss of staff morale as a result of redundancy. Finally, there are the costs associated with certain procedural aspects of the redundancy such as consultation, counselling and assistance with job search.

*Longer-term costs* Probably the main longer-term cost is the continuing loss of funds from the pension scheme. This arises because redundancy (and especially voluntary redundancy) results in an increase in the number of pensioners and a decrease in the number of contributors. Where the pension fund is in surplus, that is, has funds over and above those actuarily required, the depletion of that surplus may be reducing funds (some of) which would have been owned by the company.

A second type of longer-term cost is where the company, over a sustained period, attempts to bring alternative jobs to the area in which the redundancies occurred (as in the case of coal and steel through British Coal Enterprise and British Steel (Industry) Ltd respectively). Here the costs are those of financing a continuing organization and providing incentives for incoming firms. Where large-scale redeployment is attempted within a company, this again is likely to be a longer-term exercise.

## The benefits of redundancy

In contrast to the costs, the benefits of redundancy are easier to identify, although some are not necessarily any easier to quantify. Measurable savings flow from having a reduced level of staffing, and these are of continuing benefit. Similarly, savings from the introduction of better working practices, from the use of contractors and from organizational restructuring are of a continuing nature, although not as easily quantifiable.

As with other investments, it will be necessary to measure the flow of benefits from redundancy over a specified period in order to determine their relationship to the costs involved.

This chapter has indicated a purposive approach to redundancy whereby the requirement for fewer employees is used as a launching pad for improved organizational performance. At the same time, management will seek to minimize any post-redundancy problems. In chapter 4 such an approach is extended to include consideration of redundancy payments and procedures, agreements with unions and other matters which, taken together, may form a coherent strategy.

### Notes

1   ACAS, *Labour Flexibility in Britain*, 1987 Survey, London: Advisory, Conciliation and Arbitration Service, 1988, p. 4.
2   An integrated organization based on the concept of the flexible craftsman can reduce staffing by 20 to 30 per cent when compared with traditional departmental structures (engineering, electrical and so on). Cross, M., *Towards The Flexible Craftsman*, London: Technical Change Centre, 1985.
3   Cross, *Towards the Flexible Craftsman*, pp. 5 and 35–6. For an example of guidance on the health and safety aspects of multi-skilling in a particular industry see HSC Oil Industry Advisory Committee, *Guidance on Multi-Skilling in the Petroleum Industry*, London: HMSO, 1992. This is intended to apply, for example, where operators carry out engineering work and other support tasks such as quality control, and where maintenance craftsmen become plant operators.
4   On this subject, see Coulson-Thomas, C. and Coe, T., *The Flat Organisation: Philosophy and Practice*, British Institute of Management, 1991.
5   In the context of shortages of younger workers due to demographic factors, use of voluntary redundancy may be counter-productive. It removes valuable skills and experience by encouraging older workers

to leave under combined early-retirement/redundancy schemes. These skills may be difficult to replace when there is an upturn – young workers will be in short supply (Institute of Manpower Studies, *Corporate Employment Policies and the Older Worker*, Brighton: IMS, 1991).

6   The British Telecom case offers some lessons in this respect. The terms of the redundancy scheme were so attractive that 17,000 engineering staff volunteered for 8,000 redundancies and 7,000 clerical staff volunteered for 2,000 redundancies. Sixteen thousand employees wanting to leave were told that they would have to stay. According to the unions this provoked fury among BT's employees and further demoralized an already insecure workforce. The National Communications Union claimed that some of its members had already bought businesses, put their homes on the market or made plans to emigrate. BT said it had made clear that ultimately each redundancy would be a management decision. It said that people should not have made firm plans until the company had made them a firm offer which they accepted. See *Financial Times*, 7 July 1992.

7   Turnbull discusses this issue in the context of the redundancies of the 1980s: Peter J. Turnbull, Leaner and Possibly Fitter: the Management of Redundancy in Britain, *Industrial Relations Journal*, Vol. 19, no. 3 (autumn 1988) pp. 201–13.

# 4

# A Strategy for Managing Redundancy

A strategic approach to redundancy supposes that management is proactive rather than reactive. How does such an approach fit within the concept of human resource management? What are the advantages and disadvantages of entering into a redundancy agreement with a trades union? What issues might arise when trying to implement a redundancy strategy? These are questions addressed in the present chapter which begins by describing the different types of approach.

## Redundancy Policy and Human Resource Management

### Types of approach

In the early days of the statutory RP scheme (and therefore prior to the operation of the law of unfair dismissal or the redundancy procedure requirements of the Trade Union and Labour Relations (Consolidation) Act (TULR(C)A)), firms in the private sector were reluctant to draw up redundancy policies in advance of the occurrence of redundancy.[1] In contrast, such policies were common in local and central government and in the nationalized industries, and most of these were the product of negotiations with trades unions.[2] Since that time the adoption of redundancy policies has become more widespread and ACAS's 1986 survey (in which 89 per cent of the establishments were in the private sector) found that 70 per cent of establishments had written arrangements and nearly 50 per cent of establishments had agreements with trades unions.[3] The sample was based on the pattern of ACAS's work and may not be representative in the strict sense of the term, but two things are clear. First, the existence of redundancy policies (in advance of the occurrence of redundancy) is now more common; and second, there is an increasing tendency to formalize policies by committing them to paper.

Employers may take three broad types of approach to redundancy.[4] As noted, historically (at least in the private sector) there has been an ad hoc approach where no policy is determined until the advent of redundancy. The practice adopted then would depend upon the circumstances of the case. A second type of approach would be to have a formal policy, that is, a statement by management of the ways in which the organization proposes to deal with redundancy should it arise. The third type of approach is to determine policy jointly with one or more trades unions, and to set it out in a formal agreement. The arguments for and against having a redundancy agreement with a trades union are considered later (pp. 55–6); the immediate question is why an employer should have a redundancy policy at all, except at the time redundancy arises.

### *Reasons for having a redundancy policy in advance of redundancy*

In broad terms, the application of a HRM philosophy is likely to lead to a company adopting a policy for redundancy. Such a philosophy argues for the most effective use of human potential in an organization, recognizing that people are the source of that organization's competitive edge in the market. A HRM philosophy also demands that human resource decisions are based on a sound contribution being made to overall business goals. A policy for redundancy is likely to help an organization plan and use its human resources most effectively and deal with change in a way which focuses sharply upon the needs of the business. Therefore, it helps apply two fundamental principles of the wider HRM strategy.

In more practical terms, it is inevitable that an employer from time to time will need to adjust his demand for labour in response to external factors. Therefore, a policy for dealing with such an adjustment will be necessary at some stage. The issue is whether there is something to be gained from having that policy already in place before a redundancy occurs.[5] The first argument is that disputes over redundancy are related to the way redundancy is handled rather than the existence of redundancy *per se* or the scale of redundancies. A policy developed in advance, with some thought and planning, may make it easier for management to handle a difficult situation. Second, a particularly important aspect of the handling of redundancy may be consultation, especially in unionized workplaces. An employer who consults will need to start doing so as soon as possible (in law 'at the earliest opportunity'),[6] and will need to plan the consultation exercise. In effect, this requires there to be at least some element of policy determined in advance.

Next, redundancy may present a big opportunity for organizational change, for example, for work restructuring or alterations to the management structure. Management may benefit by knowing in advance the changes they wish to make, and how these might be made if redundancy occurs. Finally, redundancy may be a deliberate (and perhaps continuing) policy rather than something which occurs and requires a response. It may be a policy to be operated over a period of years with a view to the restructuring of the organization, as, for example in newly privatized firms dealing with their inherited overstaffing. On the other hand, the context of redundancy may vary, and any policy will need to be flexible enough to be operated effectively in different situations. Moreover, communicating the policy to employees and/or unions may create a fear that redundancies are imminent. Also, there are some separate arguments about the wisdom of agreements with unions in advance of redundancy.

If the evidence tends to support the idea of a redundancy policy worked out in advance, what should be the objectives of such a policy and what should the policy contain in order to meet those objectives? The objectives should relate clearly to business performance. Thus, it should be the aim of a redundancy policy to minimize the disruption arising from the reduction in demand for labour, whether caused by union opposition or post-redundancy dislocation. Second, the policy should assist the company in maintaining its good reputation. Third, it must minimize the likelihood of infringement of the law and legal challenges. Finally, it should act as a vehicle for improving the performance of the organization – through increased productivity or a more effective structure, for example.

The contents of a policy which has such objectives might include:

- steps to minimize redundancies;
- consultation arrangements;
- selection criteria and methods;
- extra-statutory redundancy payments; and
- other measures such as time off to look for a new job, assistance with job search and counselling.

(See chapters 7, 8 and 9 for more detailed discussion of the various policy components.)

## *The costs and benefits of redundancy*

If redundancy is to be approached as an investment, policy issues will have to be dealt with in advance in order to determine the initiatives management will need to take. For example, questions about the amount of resources to be applied, the use of voluntary redundancy and early retirement, the extent of consultation and assistance, human resource planning and the changes to be introduced by means of redundancy will all need addressing in advance if the redundancy is to be handled effectively. A redundancy policy is a prerequisite of such an approach.

## Agreements with Trades Unions

### *Advantages and disadvantages of agreements*

Before considering whether it is in management's interest to enter into a redundancy agreement with a trades union, it is worth noting that a union may not want such an agreement. Historically this is because many unions have a formal policy of opposition to redundancy, and view agreements in advance of redundancy as a surrender of this principle. Increasingly, however, unions are accepting that in practice redundancies will occur, and that the best option is to have an agreement which provides for consultation and offers protection against compulsion and unfair selection.[7]

An important advantage of having a redundancy agreement is the probability of reduced union opposition to redundancy. This occurs because agreements will usually address unions' chief anxieties, viz: compulsion, lack of consultation and unfair selection. A second advantage is that a redundancy agreement may be a way of securing greater co-operation from unions over matters such as the introduction of new technology or new working practices.[8] An agreement offers a union a degree of security, for example by including steps to be taken to minimize redundancies, and by doing so encourages a less oppositional stance by the union in relation to matters of change. A third advantage is that a redundancy agreement may facilitate better human resource planning.

There are, however, some considerations to be weighed in the balance. First, employers sometimes shy away from redundancy agreements in advance because they feel that they will be agreeing to a floor of redundancy rights which unions will try to build upon at the time of redundancy. This point is of particular importance in relation to redundancy payments. Second, some employers feel that by settling redundancy terms in advance, when a trades union may have more influence than it might have at the time of redundancy, they may pay more than is necessary. An advance agreement on redundancy may offer more protection to the union and its members than it could obtain by negotiation at the time of redundancy.

In addition, there are legal implications. Where there is an agreement, an employee selected for redundancy in contravention of the agreement will be held to be automatically unfairly dismissed unless the employer had 'special reasons' for departing from the agreement (see chapter 7). Selection will also be automatically unfair if it is made in contravention of a 'customary arrangement'.[9]

Moreover, there is the complex and potentially expensive problem of whether redundancy terms and procedures agreed with a trades union can be the basis of an action in contract: that is, does the collective agreement on redundancy (or any part of it) become incorporated into the contracts of employment of individual employees. If it does, employees may be able to claim damages for breach of contract or seek an injunction to prevent a breach should management attempt to change terms or procedures. This can create problems for management if, when redundancy does occur, they cannot or do not wish to stand by the terms agreed.

A collective agreement is presumed not to be legally enforceable, but this does not prevent its terms being enforceable by individuals where those terms have become incorporated (*Marley* v. *Forward Trust Group Ltd*). This process is shown in figure 4.

Redundancy terms and procedures can also be expressly agreed as part of the contract of employment, that is, without reference to any collective agreement. The policy implications of legally-enforceable redundancy arrangements are discussed below (see pp. 61–4).

## Contents of redundancy agreements

The Institute of Personnel Management recommends careful consideration of the benefits of a redundancy procedure agreement.[10]

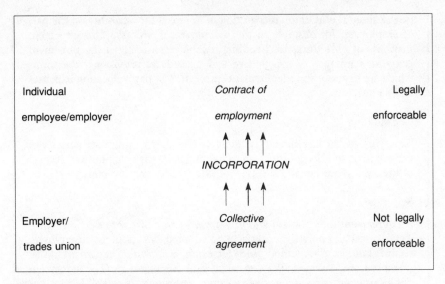

**Figure 4** Collective agreements on redundancy and their relationship to the contract of employment

Typically, the contents of such agreements might include some or all of the following.[11]

---

Contents of a Redundancy Procedure Agreement

Preamble

The preamble to a redundancy agreement usually contains statements of intent and responsibility such as:

- management's commitment to the objective of employment security through effective business and human resource planning;
- management's responsibility for the viability of the organization, recognizing that in certain circumstances redundancies may be unavoidable; and
- a management undertaking that unions will be consulted and jointly-agreed procedures followed.

Measures for avoiding or minimizing redundancy

This section of an agreement might include a management commitment to avoid compulsory redundancy as far as is possible, and an undertaking to consult unions at the earliest practicable time, giving details of those at risk from redundancy. It may contain a management undertaking to jointly consider the various means of avoiding or minimizing redundancy (see chapter 1) and union recognition of the need for flexibility on the part of employees, for example in the redeployment process. The agreement may set out procedures for handling redeployment, and (if the agreement contains a mixture of substantive and procedural provisions) the terms which are to apply on redeployment (protection of pay; relocation expenses and so on).

### Consultation

This part of the agreement is likely to lay down minimum periods of consultation and the information to be disclosed. (See chapter 8 in respect of the legal requirements and typical extra-statutory provisions.)

### Selection

An agreement may contain a jointly-agreed procedure for selection which would cover not only the criteria to be adopted (for example, disciplinary record) but also the method used (for example, how that record would be measured and assessed in a consistent and fair manner). The agreement might provide for a review of selection decisions to establish that the criteria are being applied properly. In *Williams and ors* v. *Compair Maxam Ltd*, the EAT stated that an employer should try to agree selection criteria with a union, and adopt criteria capable of objective interpretation.

### Early retirement

Agreements will usually provide for early retirement since this is an important way of avoiding compulsory redundancy. The agreement may not go beyond a general commitment to using the method but on the other hand it may also include substantive matters, that is, the terms themselves. Typically, early retirement will be available from 55, but sometimes 50, with a degree of enhancement of pensionable service. For anyone aged 60 or more the enhancement is likely to increase their pensionable service to what it would have been had they worked until 65, assuming that this was the normal retiring age. For anyone below 60, the enhancement is likely to be less but may increase with age.

### Other aspects

An agreement may contain provisions relating to:

- time off to look for a new job or to arrange training (This is a legal requirement (see chapter 8).);
- assistance with job search;
- counselling;
- recall and re-engagement, that is, recalling redundant employees when there are future vacancies, giving them priority over other applicants and perhaps providing a measure of continuity of employment (although continuity will have been broken for statutory RP purposes if they received a statutory RP).

Appeals and hardship

There is often a procedure under which individuals can appeal against their selection for redundancy or apply when there is particular hardship.

Review, termination and interpretation

This part of the agreement would include details of any periodic review of the agreement and the procedure for its termination. It might also specify where the agreement could be departed from or applied flexibly. This is particularly important in view of the provisions in s. 59 of the EP(C)A (see below, pp. 96–8).

As already indicated, a redundancy agreement may confine itself to procedural matters or may also extend to include substantive provisions such as notice periods, fringe benefits and severance payments. In relation to the last of these items, the agreement may say how RPs are to be calculated, and how overtime, commission, accrued holiday pay and accumulated time off in lieu are to be treated. Management may feel that a procedure agreement worked out in advance will be of some benefit, but that substantive terms are best settled when there is a redundancy in the light of the conditions applying at the time.

## Implementing the Policy

### *The use of voluntary redundancy*

Management may tend to use VR where it expects that unions would oppose compulsory redundancies and cause the organization to incur costs such as those which might result from industrial action[12] or union involvement in decision-making. The latter may prevent management from taking commercially necessary decisions or delay those decisions. Compulsory redundancy may also result in costs because of damage to corporate image. Such costs can include increased difficulty in recruiting and retaining suitable staff, reduced morale and commitment of staff and diminished product demand. Where the organization is in the public sector, costs may be incurred in the form of loss of political support.

VR has implications for the mode of redundancy decision-making and the relative influence of the parties. In particular it causes a shift in the locus of power from management and union to management and individual employee. A main implication of this is increased power for management *vis-à-vis* union. Voluntary redundancy emphasizes employee/employer harmony at the expense of union influence. It does this by giving the employee more say and by offering the prospect of a mutually acceptable alternative to continued employment. It also provides the method by which the outcome can be achieved, viz: individual bargaining. In this way, redundancy tends to become accepted through a series of individual decisions and the prospect of it being challenged collectively is diminished. This can be seen as reflecting an extension of freedom to contract because it permits employees and employers to contract with each other over an issue which in a unionized setting normally would be settled by collective bargaining. The ability of a union to oppose redundancy is reduced if a substantial proportion of its members wishes to accept redundancy and would not take part in industrial action to oppose it. Intra-union tensions may be created because some members wish to accept redundancy and some wish to oppose it. The above 'individualization' thesis suggests that VR can be used to transfer the locus of power from the collective to the individual level, and so weaken the influence of trades unions. Overall, VR will be used where its perceived costs are less than the perceived costs of using compulsory redundancy.

Experience of using VR suggests a generally favourable rate of take-up[13] even in areas of high unemployment. Take-up is likely to be particularly favourable if there are substantial numbers of people in the age-group which has entitlement to an early, enhanced pension. This supposes that the organization has an occupational pension scheme and that the scheme provides for early, enhanced pensions. It may be that this makes the use of VR more likely in large organizations than in small ones. Take-up will also tend to be greater where earnings are relatively high and service relatively long, since these are factors which lead to higher RPs. A major requirement will be the availability of finance to allow RPs in excess of the statutory amount.[14] An unfavourable redundancy context, such as one where working practices are being changed, may encourage people to volunteer and a redundancy which does not involve the complete closure of a site may make it easier to accommodate those who wish to stay. Take-up is likely to be better if there is an absence of union opposition to VR or if the union is unable to exert sufficient control over its members to prevent them from volunteering. Where take-up is inadequate, management might be able to increase it by improving the redundancy package (or marketing it more effectively) or by putting pressure on individuals or groups.

It is expected that in using VR, management will not only want to bring forward the required number of volunteers, but will also want to control the timing of departures and to minimize the problems of adjustment in the post-redundancy period. The most successful VR exercises are likely to have management control over these issues. There are a number of ways of controlling the timing: for example, specifying a reasonable period within which the redundancy will occur (such as six months, with the decision on timing left to management); and providing financial incentives or penalties, including reduced RPs for late volunteers. As regards post-redundancy adjustment, management will want to ensure that the retained workforce has the required skills and experience.[15] Therefore, management may find it more effective to select carefully among volunteers or to use a targeted invitation to volunteer (or both) than to allow the self-selection that results from uncontrolled volunteering and largely unrestricted acceptance of VR applications.

In the above circumstances, VR would be an effective technique for dealing with staff reduction. In a unionized setting its use allows a degree of honour on both sides; it can be said to be in the tradition of industrial relations compromise. The union has not failed in its duty by abandoning any individual member, and the employer has not behaved irresponsibly in the search for economies by forcing anyone to go. However, VR may also be of use in non-unionized organizations if corporate image is likely to be damaged by the use of compulsory redundancy and costs result from this.

## Negotiations and consultations

There is a legal requirement to consult recognized, independent trades unions and a failure to consult individual employees may amount to unreasonableness in the context of an unfair dismissal claim. However, there is no requirement to negotiate, although the TURERA requires that consultation shall be undertaken with a view to reaching agreement).

What can be said about the mechanics of gaining acceptance of redundancy in a unionized setting? First, the method of handling redundancy may be more important than the scale of job loss or the fact of redundancy. Compulsion, unfair selection and lack of consultation appear to be the main sources of potential opposition. Second, there may be various possibilities for bypassing or at least reducing the significance of collective bargaining and reducing union influence. The adoption of VR has this effect but there are other means such as the counselling of employees and direct communication more generally. Third, the role of finance is likely to be important. It may dissuade people from opposing compulsory redundancy, or make it possible for people to volunteer where voluntary redundancy is used.

Managers may hold differing views about the wisdom of a redundancy agreement (in advance of redundancy) which includes terms as well as procedures. Much depends upon perceptions of relative bargaining power and ideas about what is most effective strategically. The level(s) at which redundancy negotiations are conducted is another strategic issue, depending upon perceptions of how bargaining power is distributed at different levels, upon corporate structure and upon the subject matter to be negotiated. There is likely to be some merit in controlling the strategic and financial aspects of redundancy from above, thus providing a framework for local bargaining.[16] Where redundancy is being used as a vehicle for improving productivity it will be necessary to negotiate the detailed changes at a local level, but if bargaining becomes too decentralized it may get out of control. In non-union settings the situation clearly is much simpler.

### Changing redundancy terms or procedures

What if there exists a prior agreement on redundancy procedure, or indeed, an agreement concerning both terms and procedures, but management wish to depart from it?[17] For example, suppose an agreement had been made which included a commitment to LIFO as the selection method, this agreement dating from a period when the union's influence was much stronger than it is today. What if management wish to select on the basis of factors such as skills, experience, training, or work performance? As noted earlier, the agreement itself is unlikely to be legally enforceable, but a critical issue will be whether the agreement (or part of it) has become incorporated into individual contracts of employment, so giving individual employees the right of legal action.

The rules about incorporation are relatively straightforward but the results of their application can be uncertain. First, however, it has to be stated that the problem cannot be solved simply by ter-minating the collective agreement: this does not remove incorporated terms from individual contracts. Even though the agreement has ceased to exist, the terms which were incorporated remain in indi-vidual contracts and can be the basis for legal actions (*Robertson* v. *British Gas Corporation*). (This would be the case only where the collective agreement or one or more of its terms was unilaterally varied, abrogated or withdrawn by management. Where there was consensual variation of collectively-agreed terms, the incorporated terms would also be varied.)

Where the employee alleges breach of contract because the em-ployer has not been bound by a provision in a redundancy agreement, the employee will have to prove that there has been incorporation and then establish that the alleged breach occurred. Conversely, an employer may defend such a case by showing that incorporation did not occur, or that if it did there was no breach of contract. A term in the agreement allowing for departure from the agreement or its flexible application would help in respect of the latter argument.

Incorporation can be express or implied. The former would in-volve there being an express term of the contract which stated that specified matters would be as negotiated from time to time with one or more trades unions. The process can apply equally to procedures, so that there is nothing in principle to prevent a redundancy pro-cedure agreement being incorporated, and therefore legally enforce-able by the individual employee (*Alexander and ors* v. *Standard Telephones and Cables Ltd (No. 2)*). The legal tests used to deter-mine implied terms involve ascertaining the intentions of the parties or implying what is necessary to make the contract workable in practice. It has been suggested that custom can be the basis for incorporation.[18] To be incorporated, terms and procedures will have to be apt – precise enough to be incorporated and couched in terms of an individual rather than a purely collective right. In *British Leyland UK Ltd* v. *McQuilken* the terms of a redundancy procedure were *not* incorporated: the agreement was about policy rather than individual rights. In contrast, the Court of Appeal held in *Marley* that a six-month trial period for redeployment, provided for in a collective agreement, *was* incorporated and was legally enforceable. The contract of employment incorporated a personnel manual which included the terms of the collective agreement.

Where there is incorporation and a breach of a contractual term, an employer will need to approach the question of changing re-dundancy provisions in the same way as he would approach any other contractual change. The fact of non-acceptance of the change, despite consultation and the need for the change having been explained, will have to be established. Thereafter, due notice of termination of contract will be required to avoid claims that there has been a wrongful dismissal. This may be accompanied by an offer to employ under a new contract containing the changed terms. Where an employee has two years' or more qualifying employment, he or she will be able to challenge the fairness of the dismissal by applying to an industrial tribunal. An employer will be able to defend such a claim by showing that there was a real business need for the change, that this amounted to a 'substantial reason' for dismissal and that in the context of a refusal by the employee the employer behaved reasonably in dismissing.[19]

### Using the pay system

Another strategic question is whether the pay system can be used to increase acceptance of redundancy and/or enhance post-redundancy performance. Three examples are put forward to illustrate the sorts of techniques that employers have found to be successful and in all the cases the pay increases have been implemented in arrears, after the productivity improvements have been demonstrated. First, there are bonus schemes based on the value-added principle. Thus, bonus might be determined by:

$$\frac{\text{Turnover minus the cost of materials and services}}{\text{Employment costs}} \times 100$$

and is increased by anything that reduces costs or increases output. There might be a guaranteed level of bonus in exchange for the agreement itself, and then percentage increases in gross wages for specified percentage improvements in value-added. There may be extra bonus when certain value-added threshholds are reached. It is argued that such bonuses are effective motivators through increasing employee involvement and commitment.

A second approach is to link pay increases directly to job losses, for example:

- 3 per cent increase if staffing is reduced to 11,500 by a specified date;
- 4 per cent if 11,300;
- 5 per cent if 11,000; and
- 6 per cent if 10,900.

In a voluntary redundancy context some of the criticism levelled at volunteers for 'selling' jobs may be deflected because the volunteers are directly financing the wage increases of those who remain and otherwise might level the criticism.

A third way of using the pay system is to adopt a more conventional form of productivity bonus or agree a comprehensive productivity package. The former might be based on physical indices of production or milestones in relation to productivity achievement, such as X man hours per tonne. The latter can take the form of an agreement with detailed changes in working practices set out in a schedule, and may set a date by which the changes are to be achieved if the pay side of the agreement is to be implemented. A joint monitoring committee may be set up under such an agreement in order to implement the changes and review progress.

In this chapter it has been argued that a human resource management philosophy supposes a strategic approach to redundancy, in which careful attention is paid to a range of issues including the use of VR, argeements with unions (where these apply) and the operation of the pay system. All the various strands of policy examined in this and other chapters – RPs, procedures, productivity improvement and so on – can be woven into the strategy.

## Notes

1  Gennard, J., Great Britain, in Yemin, E., (Ed.), *Workforce Reductions in Undertakings*, Geneva: International Labour Office, 1982. See p. 123.
2  Yemin, *Workforce Reductions in Undertakings*.
3  ACAS, *Redundancy Arrangements*, Occasional Paper 37, London: Advisory, Conciliation and Arbitration Service, 1987, p. 24.
4  See ACAS, *Redundancy Handling*, Advisory Booklet No. 12, London: Advisory, Conciliation and Arbitration Service, 1988, p. 5.
5  It should be borne in mind that the policies of public authorities in relation to their staff might be subject to judicial review (*McLaren* v. *Home Office*). However, in *R* v. *London Borough of Hammersmith and Fulham ex parte NALGO and ors* the High Court ruled that while an individual had a private law right to apply to an industrial tribunal, there was no private law right allowing the employer's policy to be quashed. NALGO and two employees affected by the Borough's policy had applied for the decision to adopt the policy to be quashed on the

basis that it was indirectly discriminatory on grounds of sex and race.

6  Trade Union and Labour Relations (Consolidation) Act 1992, s. 188(2).

7  A survey of the largest TUC unions found that 21 out of the 25 which responded were prepared to negotiate redundancy terms (Booth, A.L., Extra-Statutory Redundancy Payments in Britain, *British Journal of Industrial Relations*, November 1987).

8  ACAS, *Redundancy Arrangements*, p. 25.

9  EP(C)A 1978, s. 59.

10  Institute of Personnel Management, *The IPM Redundancy Code*, London: IPM, 1991, p. 6.

11  See: The IPM Redundancy Code, pp. 6–7; ACAS, *Redundancy Handling*, pp. 23–5; and Bourn, C., *Redundancy Law and Practice*, London: Butterworths, 1983, pp. 276–307.

12  This may mean that VR is likely to be used where redundancies are large-scale and generalized if this implies that the potential for industrial action would be greater in the event of compulsory redundancy. However, the evidence tends to suggest that the manner of redundancy is the key issue, rather than its scale.

13  In the British Telecom Release 92 case over half of the 200,000 workforce expressed an interest. There were 62,500 applications (31 per cent) of which 46,000 were said to be serious (23 per cent).

14  However, there is a danger of over-financing a voluntary redundancy scheme. See above, pp. 31–2.

15  This may need to be determined at site or company level whereas some aspects of VR (for example, work adjustments) may require decisions at a lower level.

16  In a survey of enterprises with over 1,000 employees, it was found that decisions on redundancy terms tend to be more centralized than those on some other industrial relations policy questions affecting establishments, for example, numbers employed (Edwards, P., Marginson, P., Purcell, J. and Sisson, K., *The Management of Industrial Relations in Large Enterprises*, Warwick Papers in Industrial Relations, No. 11, Coventry: University of Warwick, 1991.)

17  Two current examples of this are at GEC and British Coal. In the former case, unions are claiming that GEC has gone back on redundancy agreements negotiated at divisional level by imposing a uniform, company-wide package in 1991 and, presumably, in the process causing breaches of contract. The effect is claimed to be a substantial reduction in the level of payments and it is thought that if the company has to meet the various claims the sum could amount to over £1 million. In the British Coal case the corporation wishes to bypass the industry's colliery closure review procedure (which can delay closures by as much as nine months) in respect of the closures announced in October 1992. Since British Coal is a public body with a statutory duty to consult its

employees, its decision to bypass the closure procedure may be subject
to judicial review. A successful application has been made (see below,
p. 126).

18  Upex, R., (General Editor), *Encyclopedia of Employment Law*, London:
Sweet and Maxwell, Edinburgh: W. Green, 1992, pp. 1433–4.

19  EP(C)A, s. 57. In terminating contracts, employers should be aware
that there may be contractual requirements in addition to the giving of
notice: for example, there may be a contractual disciplinary procedure.
A failure to meet such a contractual requirement will not only have a
bearing on reasonableness in any unfair dismissal case but will also re-
open the possibility of there being a wrongful dismissal (that is a
dismissal not in accordance with the terms of the contract) – the very
thing that termination with due notice is designed to avoid.

# Part II
# The Legal Framework

# 5
# What is Redundancy?

## The Concept of Redundancy

Redundancy is not only a human resource management phenomenon but also a legal concept. However, the same meaning is usually given to the term by managers and lawyers alike. In law, redundancy is defined as a dismissal which is 'attributable wholly or mainly to' either:

a  an actual or intended cessation of business, either generally or in the place in which the employee is employed, or
b  an actual or expected diminution in the requirements of the business for employees to carry out 'work of a particular kind', either generally or in the place in which the employee is employed.[1]

The cessation of work or diminution in requirements can be temporary or permanent.[2]

The above definition causes few problems where a whole business closes or where a site closes and the employee contractually can be required to move elsewhere in the company. Where a site closes and the employee is under no contractual duty to move, there will be a redundancy unless an offer of alternative employment (which meets the legal requirements) is accepted. An unreasonable refusal of an offer of suitable alternative employment will lose the employee his or her right to a statutory redundancy payment. Where there is no closure, partial or total, the test is whether the employer requires fewer employees to carry out 'work of a particular kind'.

The most difficult case here is where the employer does not require fewer employees in aggregate, but wants fewer to carry out one particular type of work and more to carry out another. Whether changes in technology, systems and duties amount to a change in the 'particular kind' of work will be a matter of fact and degree for the industrial tribunal. The replacement of a plumber by a heating technician *was* a redundancy. The 'particular kind' of work done by plumbers was different from that done by heating technicians (*Murphy* v. *Epsom College*). On the other hand, the replacement of an older barmaid by a younger one, in the context of the refurbishment of a public house, was not (*Vaux and Associated Breweries Ltd* v. *Ward*). The type of work was still barmaids' work. Redundancy will not be the reason for dismissal where there is a background of work changes if the dismissal does not arise out of the changes. In *Hindle* v. *Percival Boats Ltd* there was a change in technology but the dismissal was on grounds of capability which did not stem from the change.

Three important preliminary points need to be made about the position of redundancy in law. First, it should be noted that redundancy is a form of dismissal. In industrial life a distinction is often drawn between dismissal (that is, the sack, for, say, misconduct) and redundancy, which by implication is not seen as dismissal. In law, dismissal is the umbrella concept covering termination by the employer. Redundancy is one form of dismissal. The fact that a redundancy is voluntary will not prevent it from being a redundancy in law as long as the termination is by means of dismissal, rather than by mutual agreement (*Burton, Allton and Johnson Ltd* v. *Peck*). Retirement under an early retirement scheme is likely to be a mutual termination (*Birch and Humber* v. *The University of Liverpool*) but termination as a result of volunteering under a redundancy scheme should be a redundancy, even if there is early payment of retirement benefits (see below, pp. 155–6, with respect to the tax position).

Second, the key to the definition of redundancy is not the fact that the amount of work has diminished, but rather that the employer requires fewer employees. The test for redundancy, therefore, is whether fewer employees are needed. Three types of situation were specified by the Court of Appeal in *McCrea* v. *Cullen and Davidson Ltd*:

a   the work has diminished, so fewer employees are needed;
b   the work has *not* diminished, but new technology has reduced the demand for employees;
c   the work has *not* diminished, but reorganization leads to fewer employees being wanted (that is, past overstaffing).

All of the above situations constitute redundancy. In general, the redundancy test of fewer employees has been applied to the jobs being done by those made redundant. The exception has been the practice of bumping or indirect redundancy, where if a particular job is to go, the occupant might move to another job, and the person so displaced be made redundant (*W. Gimber and Sons Ltd* v. *Spurrett*). The Court of Appeal has ruled, however, that the fewer employees test should be applied to the work that could be done under the contract rather than to the job actually being done (*Haden Ltd* v. *Cowen*). Thus how widely or narrowly 'work of a particular kind' is defined may depend upon how widely or narrowly the contract terms are drawn.

A third factor of considerable importance is that the law accepts redundancy as a legitimate management decision. As noted in chapter 7, redundancy is one of the specified fair reasons for dismissal in the statute containing the unfair dismissal provisions. Essentially, the redundancy decision is a management prerogative and in the absence of bad faith there will normally be no challenge to it (*Moon and ors* v. *Homeworthy Furniture (Northern) Ltd*). Altogether this means that there is no check in law on management dismissing for the reason of redundancy, providing that redundancy is the real reason for the dismissal and that the procedure adopted conforms to the legal requirements (see chapter 7). An exception to this occurs in the realm of public law. The redundancy decision of a public body may be quashed on judicial review, as was the case when Liverpool City Corporation set an illegal rate in 1985 (*R* v. *Liverpool City Corporation ex parte Ferguson and Smith*). In the field of private law, an employee may seek an injunction to prevent redundancy but is unlikely to succeed unless there are some special factors at work. There were no such factors in *Alexander and ors* v. *Standard Telephones and Cables Ltd (No. 2)*. A relevant question in applying the balance of convenience test would be whether there was any work for the employee to do.[3]

## Meaning of Employee

It should be noted that redundancy is defined so as to apply to employees. Therefore, the legislation applies to employees but not to other types of worker, such as a self-employed person. An employee is defined as 'an individual who has entered into or works under (or where the employment has ceased, worked under) a contract of employment'. A contract of employment means 'a contract of service or apprenticeship'.[4] Unfortunately this does not get us very far, since the critical question – how is it to be decided if the worker is employed under a contract of service? – is left unanswered. In fact the common law of contract and recent case law provide some tests to be applied, although no single test is generally conclusive. The issue is whether the worker is an employee, working for an employer under a contract of employment (or service), or a person in business on his or her own account providing services for a customer under a contract for services. (A worker's contract does not have to be one of these. Depending on the facts, a middle road is possible, that is, 'a contract of its own kind' (*sui generis* – see *Ironmonger* v. *Movefield Ltd*; *Construction Industry Training Board* v. *Labour Force Ltd*). Industrial tribunals should consider the following:

- Who has the right to control the manner of work? (The control test).
- Is the worker integrated into the structure of the organization? (The organizational test).
- Whose business is it – who takes the risks, who takes the profits? (The entrepreneurial test).
- Who provides the tools, instruments and equipment? (However, some employees by custom provide their own tools).
- Is the employer entitled to exclusive service?
- Are there wages, sick pay and holiday pay? If yes, who pays them? A fixed payment for a specified period suggests a contract of employment. Payment by task argues for a contract for services, but not conclusively.
- Who has the power to: select and appoint; dismiss; fix the place and time of work; fix the time of holidays?
- Is there a mutual obligation – the employee to work, the employer to provide it? (*Nethermere (St Neots) Ltd* v. *Gardiner and Taverna*).
- What contractual provisions are there?
- Is there a duty of personal service?
- What arrangements are there for tax and National Insurance, for example, is tax deducted via PAYE?
- Is the relationship genuinely one of self-employment or is there an attempt to avoid protective legislation?

If all the relevant circumstances are considered, the matter is one of fact for the tribunal to decide, and can be appealed only if there is an error of law (*O'Kelly and ors* v. *Trusthouse Forte plc*). This would include a tribunal coming to a conclusion that no reasonable tribunal could have come to on the evidence before it. The House of Lords has ruled, however, that where a written contract determines the relationship the issue is a matter of law (*Davies* v. *Presbyterian Church of Wales*). The tribunal will examine and decide the real nature of the relationship on the facts even if the parties have themselves agreed, for example, that the worker is self-employed (*Oyston Estate Agency Ltd* v. *Trundle*).

Home-workers are not self-employed by virtue of working from home (see *Nethermere* – home-workers who were employees). Indeed, home-working is now becoming more widespread because of information technology, so that home-workers include managerial and technical staff as well as the more traditional makers of cuddly toys and garment repairers. To determine whether home-workers are employees or working under contracts for services it is necessary to apply the normal range of tests.

It should be noted that what a tribunal decides is a contract of service for employment legislation purposes may not be so for Inland Revenue purposes. Definitions of employee and self-employed may differ between the two.

## Reorganization

It is important to distinguish the concepts of redundancy and reorganization. The latter is a common occurrence in industry but is not a concept to be found in employment law. The legal implications of reorganization, if there are any, will depend upon the facts of the particular case. Thus, reorganization may involve redundancy, which is governed by legal rules, but equally, it may not. It may involve a change of employer – where there is a substantial amount of law – but equally it may not. It may involve changes in terms and conditions of employment, where a key consideration is likely to be what is permitted under the terms of the contract of employment. Where reorganization results in short-time working or lay-offs there are separate provisions.

One of the most common features of a reorganization is a change in work practices. This may involve increased flexibility of tasks, hours of work or location, but does such reorganization constitute a redundancy? The purpose of such changes is often to reduce unit costs and a major component of the saving is usually employment costs. If that is achieved by employing fewer people, the reorganization involves redundancy. Two cases illustrate the distinction which needs to be made. Reorganization was not a redundancy in *Johnson and anor* v. *Nottinghamshire Combined Police Authority* because although there were changes in terms – hours of work – no fewer employees were required. In contrast, reorganization was a redundancy in *Bromby and Hoare Ltd* v. *Evans and anor* where employees were replaced by self-employed contractors. The employer required fewer employees. Consequently redundancy legislation was brought into play in the latter case.

## Notes

1 EP(C)A, s. 81(2). The business of the employer and any associated employer(s) is to be treated as one unless (a) or (b) on page 71 above is satisfied without the need for doing so. The same principle is applied to the activities of local authorities and school governors in respect of schools maintained by the local authority (s. 81(2A)).
2 EP(C)A, s. 81(3).
3 The balance of convenience test is used to determine whether or not an injunction should be granted. See: Lewis, P., *Practical Employment Law: A Guide for Human Resource Managers*, Oxford: Blackwell, 1992, p. 83.
4 EP(C)A, s. 153.

# 6

# Changes of Employer

## The Legal Context

The common law position is that a change of employer automatically terminates the contract of employment because the contract is viewed as involving personal service. The employee would not be transferred between employers unless there was express agreement by the parties (*Nokes* v. *Doncaster Amalgamated Collieries Ltd*). The terms, and any continuity, would be a matter for agreement between the parties. If the employee joined the new employer on the condition that continuous employment with his previous employer was to count with the new employer, this could amount to a contractual promise, since the employee was not obliged to work for the new employer. An employer's subsequent refusal to abide by what was agreed would leave the door open for the employee to claim in respect of breach of contract.

In practice, changes of employer may be covered by one or more of the statutory provisions.[1] These form a complex area of law which contains a mixture of legislation, some pre-dating the UK's membership of the European Community and some deriving from it. The first issue which needs to be established is whether the change of employer is within the legislation's coverage, and in this respect it is important to note that there is no change of employer when there is a company takeover by means of share acquisition. The company, albeit owned by (and more importantly, controlled by) different people, is still the employer. This is because of the principle of corporate personality, whereby the company has a separate identity from that of its shareholders (*Salomon* v. *A. Salomon & Co. Ltd*). Since in law there is no change of employer, there is no interruption to continuity of employment for contractual or statutory purposes. If

there is a reorganization or a redundancy, actions constituting unfair
dismissal and/or breach of contract will need to be avoided as in any
normal case, but legislation relating to changes of employer will not
apply.

Some of that legislation is found in the Employment Protection
(Consolidation) Act 1978 (EP(C)A), and applies to a number of
specific types of change. Section 151 and Schedule 13 deal with
how to compute a period of employment and paragraph 17 of that
schedule is concerned with changes of employer. The effect of these
EP(C)A provisions is to protect continuity of employment for the
purpose of entitlement to statutory rights (for example, the right to
receive a statutory redundancy payment (RP)). The EP(C)A also
creates a presumption in favour of continuity, but not apparently
where there is a change of employer (*Secretary of State for Employment* v. *Cohen and Beaupress Ltd*). The provisions do not transfer
contractual rights.

## Changes of Employer other than Business Transfers

One of the types of situation covered by the EP(C)A is where there is
a change of employer brought about by Act of Parliament.[2] This
might happen, for example, where there was restructuring of a
public service such as local government. Another type of situation
is where the employer dies.[3] Under common law the contract of
employment would be ended by the death because the contract is
held to be of a personal nature. The EP(C)A extends the contract
for statutory purposes to cover employment by the personal representatives or trustees of the deceased. Moreover, continuity can be
preserved – that is, there will be no dismissal – if there is renewal or
re-engagement by the personal representatives which takes effect
within eight weeks of the death.[4] In the absence of renewal of
contract or re-engagement the employee will be treated as having
been dismissed by reason of redundancy.[5]

A further type of situation covered by the EP(C)A provisions is
where there is a change in the composition of a partnership, personal
representatives or trustees. Again, common law would say that the
contract terminates upon such changes (see *Briggs* v. *Oates*) but
the EP(C)A maintains continuity.[6] There is some uncertainty about
whether a change from a partnership to a sole trader would be
covered, but in any case this might be a business transfer (see

below).[7] The EP(C)A provisions also deal with changes of employer where the employers are associated companies.[8] Association is defined in terms of control[9] rather than in terms of membership of an employers' association. Control means voting power in the general meeting and company means a limited company. Therefore, organizations such as unincorporated associations, partnerships and local authorities cannot be associated companies (*Merton London Borough Council* v. *Gardiner*),[10] although the Employment Appeal Tribunal (EAT) took a more liberal line in *Pinkney* v. *Sandpiper Drilling Ltd*. The EP(C)A provisions also cover transfers of employees between a local education authority and the governors of schools maintained by that authority, and vice versa.[11]

If there are gaps between the employment of the employee by the first and second employer in any of the situations already mentioned, the test of whether there is continuity – apart from any specific provision – is the general one. That is, does each week satisfy the appropriate hours rule – 8 or 16 hours[12] – or where there is no contract, does one of the specified statutory reasons apply (for example the occurrence of a temporary cessation of work).[13]

## Business Transfers

A considerable amount of the legislation dealing with changes of employer relates to business transfers. There are provisions in the EP(C)A[14] and there is a set of regulations under the European Communities Act 1972 – the Transfer of Undertakings Regulations 1981 (henceforth, the Transfer Regulations).[15] As with the other types of change, the EP(C)A provisions relate only to continuity for statutory purposes. The Act states that where 'a trade or business or an undertaking . . . is transferred from one person to another'[16] the period of employment of an employee employed 'at the time of the transfer' will count as employment with the transferee. The transfer does not break the continuity. 'Person' includes a body of persons, whether corporate or incorporate.[17] The EP(C)A does not define trade or undertaking but states that business includes 'a trade or profession . . . and any activity carried on by a body of persons, whether corporate or incorporate'.[18] The coverage may be wider, therefore, than that of the Transfer Regulations, which is restricted to commercial ventures (see below).

The Transfer Regulations were enacted to give effect to the 1977 EC directive on acquired rights.[19] They apply to a relevant transfer: 'a transfer from one person to another of an undertaking'.[20] The regulations apply where there is a transfer 'effected by sale or as a result of a sale, by some other disposition, or by operation of law',[21] but this does not include changes in control which arise simply from changes in share ownership. They apply to undertakings. An undertaking includes 'any trade or business . . . in the nature of a commercial venture'.[22] Deciding what is a commercial venture is a matter of first impression for the industrial tribunal (*Woodcock and ors* v. *The Committee for the time being of the Friends School, Wigton and Genwise Ltd*). The Trade Union Reform and Employment Rights Act 1993 removes the requirement for an undertaking to be a commercial venture.

In addition to the above, the EP(C)A also provides for the offer by a new owner of a business to an employee made redundant by the previous owner.[23] The effect of this, in tandem with the provision for continuity arising out of a renewal of contract or re-engagement[24] and with the agreement of the employee,[25] is to nullify the dismissal. An offer of re-engagement must be made before the end of the employment with the former owner, and the new employment (whether renewal or re-engagement) must start no later than four weeks after the end of the old employment. Thus, offers of alternative work in a redundancy can be made by the new owners as if they were the original owners. This provision relates to the change of ownership of a business 'whether by virtue of a sale or other disposition or by operation of law'.[26]

Moreover, change of ownership does not rule out the possibility of one or more owners being both an original and a new owner. Where the job offered by the new employer is different from the old one there must be a trial period (see below, pp. 135–6). If the job is not suitable, or is reasonably refused by the employee, the transferor would be liable for the RP. Where the job is suitable and unreasonably refused, no RP would be payable at all. In judging whether the new job is different and whether the employee's rejection of it is reasonable, the change of employer is to be left out of the reckoning. If the employee accepts the position with the transferee, there is no dismissal and no RP, but continuity is preserved in respect of any future statutory claims against the transferee. Continuity is preserved across gaps of up to four weeks[27] or eight weeks if the employee is re-engaged by personal representatives after the death of an employer.[28]

Whether a business transfer will be subject to employment legislation, and if so, which legislation, will depend upon a number of factors. First, it is clear that there must be a transfer of a business, rather than just a transfer of assets (*Woodhouse and Staton* v. *Peter Brotherhood Ltd*; the European Court of Justice (ECJ) confirmed this as regards the Transfer Regulations in *Spijkers* v. *Gebroeders Benedik Abattoir CV*). Moreover, the label attached to the transfer by the parties will not necessarily determine the issue – the matter has to be judged on its facts (*Kenmir Ltd* v. *Frizzell*). The transfer of goodwill often can be an important factor in distinguishing a business transfer from an asset sale, but not conclusively so, especially in the case of the transfer of franchises where the franchisor may retain the goodwill. Another indication of the transfer of a business is the transferee taking over the transferor's customers, especially if the transferor assists by providing a client and/or customer list. Other indicators are the transfer of work in progress, an agreement by the transferor not to compete with the transferee (without which there might not be goodwill) and use of the transferor's name, trademark and so on by the transferee. Clearly, the continued employment of employees and the preservation of their working environment will not necessarily indicate a business transfer.[29]

Second, the transfer can be effected by means other than a sale, for example, by the law of succession under a will or trust.[30] Next there is the question of whether the transfer must relate to a commercial venture. This restriction is expressly stated in the Transfer Regulations but does not appear in the directive to which the regulations purport to give effect, nor in the EP(C)A provisions. Therefore, it seems that the transfer of a business which is not a commercial venture still could be subject to the EP(C)A rules and to the EC directive itself.

The requirement for the business to be of a commercial nature imposes restrictions on the legislation by excluding the effect of the Transfer Regulations although there are likely to be changes and the amended regulations probably will have a wider application.[31] Other restrictions are imposed by the need for the transfer to relate to a trade, business or undertaking. Can a terminable contract for services be regarded as a business? The contracting-out of various functions to specialist firms has become commonplace, but are these functions businesses? Whether there is a business transfer is a matter of fact for an industrial tribunal to determine (*Melon* v. *Hector Powe Ltd*); the drift of the case law is that these contracts are not undertakings within the meaning of the regulations (see, for example,

*Expro Services Ltd* v. *Smith* and *Stirling* v. *Dietmann Management Systems Ltd* – both EAT),[32] but the ECJ has held that they can fall within the scope of the directive (*Watson Rask and Christensen* v. *ISS Kantineservice A/S*). The transfer of leases, involving a double transfer (back to the lessor and then from lessor to new lessee) can count as a transfer (*Foreningen af Arbejdsledere i Danmark* v. *Daddy's Dance Hall A/S*). So too can the transfer of a lease back to the lessor followed by the sale of the business to a new owner, and the rescission of a lease followed by the owner taking over the running of the business (*P. Bork International A/S (in liquidation)* v. *Foreningen af Arbejdsledere i Danmark*; *Landsorganisationen i Danmark* v. *Ny Molle Kro*). The general principle appears to be that the application of the EC directive is not precluded provided that the undertaking retains its identity as an economic unit. The EAT later upheld this principle in relation to franchises in *LMC Drains Ltd and Metro Rod Services Ltd* v. *Waugh*.

A further issue is whether a business transfer presupposes a change of ownership. The provisions of the EP(C)A which have the effect of nullifying a redundancy where the new owner renews the contract or re-engages the employee made redundant by the previous owner clearly state that they apply to a change of ownership. The other legislation does not lay this down and the case law relating to the acquired rights directive confirms that the directive is not restricted to changes in ownership. A transfer occurs where there is a change in the person operating the undertaking and accepting responsibility for the employees (*Daddy's Dance Hall*; *Ny Molle Kro*; *P. Bork*; *Berg and Busschers* v. *I.M. Besselsen*). The Trade Union Reform and Employment Rights Act makes clear that a transfer does not need to involve a transfer of property from the transferor to the transferee.

Next there is the question of whether the employee was still employed when the transfer occurred, since this is a prerequisite for continuity of employment and/or the transfer of the contract. The provisions for nullifying redundancy apply where the employee is employed 'immediately before' the change of ownership. The statutory continuity provisions apply where the employee is employed 'at the time of the transfer' and the Transfer Regulations apply where the employee is employed 'immediately before the transfer'.[33] The drift of the case law is that the transfer occurs on completion (*Brook Lane Finance Co.* v. *Bradley*). In *Macer* v. *Abafast Ltd* the EAT held that the gap between employers could be of any length as long as it 'related to the machinery of transfer'.

To avoid continuity a transferee wishing to take on the transferor's staff will need to ensure that there is a gap of one full week in order to defeat the normal continuous employment computation rules (a week in which 16 hours are worked or contracted). Four weeks will be needed to defeat the provisions which nullify redundancies. Beyond this there is the risk of the *Macer* test being applied. An employer's defence here would have to be that the gap was not related to the transfer.

Where there is a pre-transfer dismissal, the transferee will need to ensure that any notice given to the employee by the transferor does not result in the employee being employed at the time of transfer. In this respect it should be remembered that a notice period will continue the employment contract even if the employee is not required to work. It may be prudent for employers to have a term in the employment contract to allow wages in lieu of notice. Where the notice given is less than the minimum required by statute, there is a possibility that it could be extended by statute.[34] Moreover, where a dismissal is in breach of contract, the employee can at common law keep the contract alive at least as long as the notice period by not accepting the repudiation. All of these factors may result in the employee's employment being prolonged up to the point of transfer such that liabilities pass to the transferee. Another, particularly important factor is the *Litster* principle (see below).

Finally, do the Transfer Regulations transfer statutory continuity or just contractual rights, duties and liabilities?[35] There is no definitive ruling on this. If the answer were no, continuity for statutory purposes would fall to be covered by the EP(C)A provisions. If the answer is yes, the EP(C)A provisions may be otiose.[36] And are all contract terms transferred? Apparently yes, but not terms from collateral contracts (for example, a share option scheme in *Chapman and Elkin* v. *CPS Computer Group plc*). Nor, it seems, those contract terms where there is an exclusion of liability clause which is not in breach of s. 3 of the Unfair Contract Terms Act (UCTA), 1977. In *Micklefield* v. *SAC Technology Ltd* liability was excluded even in the context of a wrongful dismissal. Maternity rights are transferred and liability for tortious acts (such as negligence) committed in relation to an employee also appear to transfer (see *Secretary of State for Employment* v. *Spence and ors* on this general question). Criminal liabilities do not transfer, and occupational pension schemes are expressly excluded from automatic transfer. Protective awards do not transfer according to the EAT in *Angus Jowett & Co.* v. *The National Union of Tailors and Garment Workers*, although the failure to pay, being a matter of contract, perhaps might.

Nothing in the regulations removes the individual's right to resign and claim a fundamental breach of contract, either for unfair dismissal or common law damages purposes. However this right is circumscribed to a degree by the wording of the regulations which says that either:

- 'a substantial change is made in his working conditions to his detriment', or
- the change in identity of the employer itself is 'significant' and 'to his detriment'.

The transfer itself will not be a repudiatory breach of contract (*Newns* v. *British Airways plc*).

Collective agreements also transfer automatically, but unless specifically provided otherwise in the agreement these will not be legally enforceable. However the collective agreement terms may be incorporated into individual contracts, which can be enforced (*Marley* v. *Forward Trust Group Ltd*). Occupational pension schemes are again excluded from automatic transfer. Trades union recognition transfers automatically if the union is independent and the business preserves its autonomy. Any redundancy agreement will have been transferred automatically so in the event of a redundancy this will be relevant to the question of unfair selection.

The employer has a duty to inform and consult union representatives. These are the representatives of independent trades unions recognized by the employer. Consultation concerns employees who may be affected by a projected transfer. The information to be divulged, in writing, comprises:

- the fact of the transfer, the date and reasons;
- the legal, economic and social implications;
- measures the transferor and the transferee propose to take *vis-à-vis* the employees. If there are no measures this must be stated.

Consultation involves considering union representations and replying to them, giving reasons for the rejection of any of them. The Trade Union Reform and Employment Rights Act 1993 (TURERA) requires that consultation must be with a view to seeking agreement on the measures to be taken. As with redundancy consultation the employer may argue 'special circumstances'. Unions may complain to an industrial tribunal within three months. Compensation of up to two weeks' pay may be awarded to each affected employee on the basis of what is 'just and equitable' taking into account the seriousness of the employer's breach of duty. The Trade Union Reform and Employment Rights Act substitutes four weeks' pay and removes the employers' right to deduct from it any payments made for failure to consult over redundancy or for breach of contract during the protected period (see pp. 116–17). It should be noted that there is no time-scale for consultation under the Transfer Regulations but information should be provided 'long enough before' the transfer to allow consultations to take place.[37] There is no requirement to consult if there is no recognized trades union or if the employer does not envisage taking measures in relation to the employees in connection with the transfer.

## The Legislation's Effect on Redundancy

Where there is a redundancy in the context of a change of employer it is necessary to distinguish between situations where there is a redundancy in law (and a requirement to make a RP) and those where continuity is preserved and there is no redundancy in law (nor, therefore, any requirement to make a RP). As noted, the legislation reverses the normal common law position that a change of employer automatically terminates the contract of employment. The Transfer Regulations state expressly that the contract of employment will continue as will rights and duties under it, including continuity of employment.[38] Thus, the mere change of identity of the employer does not give an employee the right to claim a redundancy payment. As already noted, the employee's statutory rights are transferred by virtue of the EP(C)A and other provisions have the effect of nullifying a redundancy under certain conditions if a new owner renews the redundant employee's contract or re-engages him. The effect of transfer legislation on redundancy in the context of insolvency is discussed later (pp. 154–5).

A dismissal before or after a transfer will be automatically unfair if the reason is the transfer itself or something 'connected with' it,[39] but subject to whether there is 'an economic, technical or organizational reason entailing changes in the workforce'[40] (ETO), in which case the dismissal will be deemed to be for some other substantial reason under dismissal law.[41] In ETO cases liability is determined according to the principle in *Secretary of State for Employment* v. *Spence and ors.*

This makes it clear that responsibility would lie with the transferor where the 'effective date of termination' (EDT) or 'relevant date' preceded the transfer and with the transferee if it succeeded it. (These terms are defined on pages 91 and 136). The *Spence* principle would also apply to dismissals which were not connected with the transfer. By contrast, where the dismissal is connected with the transfer, but where there is no ETO reason, the rule is as stated by the House of Lords in *Litster* v. *Forth Dry Dock and Engineering Co. Ltd and anor*. This holds that where the employee has been dismissed prior to the transfer, he is to be treated as if he had not been dismissed. Any liability thus passes to the transferee.

In the absence of an ETO reason, any dismissal connected with the transfer will be automatically unfair. Automatic means that the unfair dismissal test of reasonableness (described in chapter 7) does not apply. For there to be an ETO reason, there will have to be changes in the workforce. The Court of Appeal has ruled, in *Berriman* v. *Delabole Slate Ltd*, that changes in the workforce mean a deliberate change in the numbers and functions of employees. Straightforward changes in terms and conditions, it seems, will not constitute ETO. In *Wheeler* v. *Patel and J. Golding Group of Companies* the EAT held that an ETO must relate to the conduct of the business.

There can be an ETO reason where the same employees are kept on but asked to do entirely different jobs (*Crawford* v. *Swinton Insurance Brokers Ltd*). This situation might give rise to a constructive dismissal (defined on page 90), but the correct approach is for a tribunal first to identify the employer's conduct and then, if it does amount to a constructive dismissal, decide whether or not the dismissal is fair. In general, ETO reasons must be sufficiently specified by employers (*Gateway Hotels Ltd* v. *Stewart and ors*) and the existence of a redundancy situation does not necessarily mean that redundancy is the reason for dismissal. Thus a dismissal by administrators in order to make the business more attractive to potential buyers was not dismissal for an ETO reason despite the fact that it was carried out in the context of redundancy (*UK Security Services (Midlands) Ltd* v. *Gibbons and ors*).

An ETO constitutes 'some other substantial reason' under dismissal law, and requires the normal second stage (that is, the test of reasonableness) to be entered. The onus of proof of an ETO reason lies with the employer (*Litster*). *Gorictree Ltd* v. *Jenkinson* showed that dismissal for an ETO reason prior to a transfer can simultaneously be dismissal for redundancy giving rise to entitlement to a redundancy payment. This would be true even if the applicant was re-engaged subsequently, including immediately after the transfer, by the transferee. Where the dismissal is post-transfer because the transferee requires fewer employees this can also be due to an ETO reason (*Meikle* v. *McPhail* (*Charleston Arms*)).

The relationship between business transfers and redundancy therefore is this. The transfer itself does not constitute a redundancy, but a dismissal by the transferor or transferee, connected with the transfer and because fewer employees are required, will be a redundancy. It will be a fair dismissal by constituting an ETO reason, which in turn is deemed under the regulations to be 'some other substantial reason' for dismissal under EP(C)A. All this will be subject to meeting the general unfair dismissal test of reasonableness and the specific legal requirements relating to unfair selection for redundancy (see chapter 7).

In the absence of a dismissal (constructive or direct), there will be continuity of employment and the employee will be able to count his employment with his previous employer should he ever make a statutory claim against his new employer. Any dismissal, whether or not it is connected with a transfer, where the reason is other than a requirement for fewer employees, will not be dismissal by reason of redundancy.

## Notes

1 In addition to the general statutory provisions there are specific arrangements covering particular changes, such as those involving employees being transferred from district health authorities to NHS trusts. The National Health Service and Community Care Act 1990, s. 6 establishes continuity of employment across such changes and transfers to the new employer the original employer's rights, powers, duties and liabilities under or in connection with the contract of employment. The EP(C)A (section 116) allows the termination of certain employments by statute to be treated as dismissal by reason of redundancy. The Secretary of State exercises his power through regulations and has used this section where police forces are amalgamated and an officer will not agree to transfer.

2 EP(C)A, schedule 13, para. 17(3).

3 EP(C)A, schedule 13, para. 17(4).

4 EP(C)A, schedule 12, para. 14.

5 EP(C)A, s. 93.

6    EP(C)A, schedule 13, para. 17(5). A partnership is an unincorporated association without a legal identity. Employees are employed by the association's members jointly. A change in partners is likely to be a change of employer unless there is express provision to the effect that, or it can be inferred that, the employment is with the partners as from time to time constituted (see *Briggs* v. *Oates*).

7    On this, see McMullen, J., *Business Transfers and Employee Rights*, 2nd edition, London: Butterworths, 1992, pp. 25–27.

8    EP(C)A, schedule 13, para. 18.

9    EP(C)A, s. 153(4).

10   See also *Southern Electricity Board* v. *Collins* where it was held that a collective agreement which gave continuity on movement from one electricity board to another could not override the statute under which continuity depended upon employers being associated. The boards were not associated employers and so the employee did not have continuity for statutory RP purposes. As a result, two exemptions were sought and obtained under s. 96 EP(C)A (see below, p. 145). Local authorities are not associated companies but continuity for RP purposes is preserved on transfer by the Redundancy Payments (Local Government) (Modification) Order, SI 1983/1160 as amended.

11   EP(C)A, schedule 13, para. 18A.

12   EP(C)A, schedule 13, paras. 3, 4 and 6.

13   EP(C)A, schedule 13, para. 9.

14   EP(C)A, schedule 13, para. 17(2).

15   The Transfer of Undertakings (Protection of Employment) Regulations, SI 1981/1794.

16   EP(C)A, schedule 13, para. 17(2).

17   Interpretation Act 1978, schedule 1.

18   EP(C)A, s. 153(1).

19   EC Council Directive 77/187 (of 14 February 1977) on the Approximation of the Laws of the Member States Relating to the Safeguarding of Employees' Rights in the Event of Transfers of Undertakings, Businesses or Parts of Businesses (OJ, 1977, L61).

20   Transfer Regulations, reg. 3(1).

21   Transfer Regulations, reg. 3(2).

22   Transfer Regulations, reg. 2(1) (now amended by TURERA, s. 33(2)).

23   EP(C)A, s. 94 (repealed by TURERA, s. 51 and sch. 10).

24   EP(C)A, s. 84.

25   EP(C)A, s. 94(2).

26   EP(C)A, s. 94(1).

27   EP(C)A, schedule 13, para. 11(2).

28   EP(C)A, schedule 12, para. 15. Schedule 12, para. 13 disapplies s. 94 and substitutes schedule 12, paras. 14–16. The effect is to remove the

requirement for the offer to be made before the ending of the original contract and to substitute eight weeks for four weeks.

29  See McMullen, *Business Transfers and Employee Rights*, pp. 50–54, for a fuller discussion of these issues.

30  See McMullen, *Business Transfers and Employee Rights*, p. 33.

31  In response to a recent application for judicial review of the Further and Higher Education Act 1992 by the National Association of Teachers in Further and Higher Education, the government conceded that because the Transfer Regulations were limited to commercial ventures they did not fully implement the EC's acquired rights directive. The government has remedied the matter through its Trade Union Reform and Employment Rights Act. The European Commission had threatened infringement proceedings against the UK over the same issue. Moreover, the ECJ has held recently, in *Dr Sophie Redmond Stichting* v. *Bartol and ors*, that a local authority's termination of a subsidy to a charitable foundation, causing the foundation to cease operating, and the giving of the subsidy to another charitable foundation, was a transfer falling within the scope of the directive. There had been a change in the person carrying on the business, who was responsible for the employees. The deciding criterion is whether the unit retains its identity, that is, by continuing or resuming as before. Clearly, the requirement in the British Transfer Regulations for there to be a commercial venture is inconsistent with the ECJ's interpretation of the directive.

32  However, the EAT has held that a relevant transfer *can* take place between successive contractors, even if the transfer takes effect via a third party, providing that it amounts to the transfer of a going concern. Deciding whether there is a going concern is a matter of fact for the industrial tribunal (*Curling and ors* v. *Securicor Ltd*).

33  Reg. 5(3). The directive refers to 'the date of a transfer' (art. 3). The *Spence* case (see p. ●●) referred to moment or time.

34  EP(C)A, s. 55(5).

35  Reg. 5(2).

36  See McMullen, *Business Transfers and Employee Rights*, pp. 96–99, for a discussion of this matter.

37  Reg. 10(2).

38  The effect of the regulations is to transfer contracts of employment automatically. Therefore, a collective agreement purporting to prevent some of the employees being transferred was void (*D'Urso and ors* v. *Ercole Marelli Elletromeccanica Generale SpA and ors*).

39  Reg. 8(1).

40  Reg. 8(2).

41  EP(C)A, s. 57(1)(b).

# 7

# Unfair Dismissal Aspects

It has been noted that redundancy is a form of dismissal; as a result, it is subject to the law of unfair dismissal. In practice, the most common challenge in law to an employer's redundancy decision is an unfair dismissal claim. Therefore, this chapter identifies good practice and the requirements of the law in relation to how the individual employee should be treated in a redundancy.

## Meaning of Dismissal and Effective Date of Termination

Dismissal is defined as:

- termination of the contract by the employer with or without notice;
- the expiry of a fixed-term contract without renewal;
- constructive dismissal; and
- failure to permit a woman to return to work after confinement.

A constructive dismissal is termination by the employee, with or without notice, in circumstances where the employee is entitled to terminate the contract without notice because of the employer's conduct. Redundancy can be distinguished from early retirement even though retirement benefits may be paid early in both situations. The former is a dismissal, the latter is likely to be a mutual termination (see above, p. 37). The announcement of a plant closure to union representatives or even the fixing of a closure date will not involve a dismissal unless the date of termination of the employee's contract can be ascertained (*Doble* v. *Firestone Tyre and Rubber Co. Ltd*; *International Computers Ltd* v. *Kennedy*; *Morton Sundour Fabrics Ltd* v. *Shaw*).

The effective date of termination (EDT) is when any notice expires or, if there is no notice, the actual date of termination. For the woman refused her right to return to work the dismissal is taken as having effect on the notified day of return. Where notice given by the employer is less than the statutory minimum, the EDT (for the purposes of qualifying employment for unfair dismissal and written reasons claims, and the calculation of the basic award) becomes the date on which the statutory minimum notice would have expired. In a constructive dismissal the EDT is at the end of whatever period of notice the employer would have had to give if he had dismissed on the date of the employee giving notice or terminating (whichever applied).

The EP(C)A provides that where an employee serves counter notice, to expire before the expiry of the employer's notice of termination, the 'relevant date' for RP purposes is the date of expiry of the counter notice[1] (see chapter 9). It has been held by the EAT that the same principle applies in relation to unfair dismissal claims[2] (*Thompson* v. *GEC Avionics Ltd*).

Sometimes the contract of employment can end because one party is no longer capable of performing it in the way the parties envisaged. This is called frustration. The circumstances are likely to be external, unforeseen and not the fault of either party (*Paal Wilson & Co. A/S* v. *Partenreederei Hannah Blumenthal*). Long-term illness is an example. A borstal sentence was frustration in *F.C. Shepherd & Co. Ltd* v. *Jerrom*. The contract may be said to be frustrated after the passage of time. The significance of frustration is that it is not a dismissal, therefore no question of unfair dismissal or redundancy would arise.

The expiry of a fixed-term contract is itself a dismissal. Such a contract must have definite starting and finishing dates, although there may be provision for termination by notice within its period (*British Broadcasting Corporation* v. *Dixon*). This contrasts with a task contract which is discharged by performance. Its expiry does not constitute a dismissal (*Wiltshire County Council* v. *NATFHE and Guy*).

The time limit for unfair dismissal claims is three months from the EDT, although industrial tribunals can extend this period if it is not reasonably practicable to submit the claim in time.

## Unfair Dismissal: Exclusions

The following are excluded:

- Anyone who is not an employee (see above, pp. 73–5).

- Anyone who is employed for fewer than 16 hours a week (but see below).
- Anyone who has reached normal retiring age. Where there is a normal retiring age and it is the same for men and women, that age applies even if it is different from 65. In any other case 65 will apply.[3]
- Anyone with less than two years' continuous employment with their present employer.
- Anyone who at the time of dismissal was taking part in unofficial industrial action. In effect, those taking official action are also excluded, but subject to exceptions.
- Anyone who is the subject of a certificate excepting them from the legislation in the interests of national security or confirming that they have been dismissed for that same reason.
- Anyone in a number of specified occupations, namely share fishermen, the police and the armed forces.
- Those who ordinarily work outside Great Britain.
- Those with contracts for a fixed term of one year or more who have agreed in writing to waive their rights.
- Those covered by a dismissal procedure which is exempted from the legislation by ministerial Order.
- Anyone who has made an agreement to refrain from proceeding further with or making a complaint to a tribunal 'where a conciliation officer has taken action'.[4]
- Anyone whose employment contract has an illegal purpose (for example, to defraud the Inland Revenue). An unknowingly illegal contract may not restrict statutory rights.

The legislation does apply to Crown Servants and to House of Commons staff and the TURERA extends it to cover the Armed Forces and House of Lords staff.

The hours qualification arises out of the legal definition of continuous employment.[5] An employee either must be employed for 16 hours or more per week, or work under a contract which normally involves employment for 16 hours or more. Those with five years' continuous employment enjoy continuity if the contract is for eight or more hours per week. An employee working fewer than eight hours a week will never obtain any continuous employment. Up to 26 weeks of working under a contract for eight or more but less than 16 hours are counted as continuous employment and preserve continuity if they are sandwiched between two periods of working under a contract for 16 hours or more.

Continuity is preserved for a maximum of 26 weeks during periods in which there is no contract of employment when the employee is incapable of work due to sickness or injury or absent from work because of pregnancy or confinement, and these weeks count. A woman on statutory maternity leave can enjoy continuity beyond 26 weeks. There is also continuous employment in the absence of a contract when a temporary cessation of work occurs (see *Ford* v. *Warwickshire County Council*). A temporary cessation will last only for a relatively short time, with the emphasis on relatively. The correct test to decide whether a cessation is temporary is to consider all the circumstances in the light of the whole history of employment. This includes the expectations of the parties when the absence began and the length of absence (*Flack and ors* v. *Kodak Ltd*). There can be continuous employment where, again in the absence of a contract of employment, the employee is absent from work in circumstances where by arrangement or custom he or she is regarded as continuing in employment 'for all or any purposes'.

Separate contracts with the same employer cannot be aggregated to obtain sufficient hours and therefore sufficient continuous qualifying employment (*Lewis* v. *Surrey County Council*), although there could be a global contract. Once an employee has sufficient continuous employment to qualify for an employment right, he remains qualified until he works under a contract for less than eight hours per week *and* in any week actually is employed for fewer than 16 hours. Continuous employment begins on the date specified in the contract of employment, even if this is not a working day, rather than when the employee actually starts to do the work (*General of the Salvation Army* v. *Dewsbury*).

There is no continuous employment qualification if the dismissal is for reason of race, sex, trades unionism or non-unionism, although race and sex discrimination cases would have to be taken under the Race Relations Act 1976 and Sex Discrimination Act 1975 rather than the unfair dismissal provisions of the EP(C)A in the absence of two years' continuous employment. The qualification is one month where the dismissal is on medical grounds specified in schedule 1 of the EP(C)A.

Normal retiring age (NRA) means contractual retiring age where there is one which is strictly applied. A contractual retiring age which is not strictly applied creates a presumption that the NRA is the same. In such circumstances, and also where there is no contractual retiring age at all, the overall test is the reasonable expectation of employees (*Waite* v. *Government Communications Headquarters*). The reference group for establishing NRA will be determined by the 'position' held by the employee.[6] Position means the following taken as a whole: status as an employee, nature of the work and terms and conditions (*Hughes* v. *Department of Health and Social Security*). A NRA in excess of 65 will allow unfair dismissal claims up to that NRA. This contrasts with redundancy payments where eligibility is restricted to those who have not reached 65 years even if the NRA is in excess of 65. A NRA of 60 at British Telecom meant that the company could require employees to retire at 60 or over without fear of them being able to pursue unfair dismissal claims (*Brooks and ors* v. *British Telecommunications plc*).

## The Essence of the Law of Unfair Dismissal

The essence of the law on unfair dismissal is the right of the employee not to be unfairly dismissed by his or her employer. In deciding cases, industrial tribunals go through a two-stage process. They ask: has the employer established a fair reason for the dismissal? did the employer act reasonably or unreasonably?

The starting point is to ask when a dismissal is fair, rather than when it is unfair. This is because the statute defines fairness rather than unfairness. The fair reasons for dismissal – the first stage of the process – are:

- the capability or qualifications of the employee;
- the conduct of the employee;
- the employee was redundant;
- the employee could not continue in his work without contravention of a statutory duty or restriction;
- some other substantial reason (SOSR).

A dismissal also will be fair if it can be shown that its purpose was to safeguard national security.[7] If an employer cannot establish a fair reason his or her case will fall. On the other hand, if a tribunal is satisfied that one of these reasons has been shown, it must then decide whether the employer acted reasonably or unreasonably in treating it as a sufficient reason for dismissal. The second stage of the process therefore, is a test of reasonableness. The statute says little about reasonableness except that tribunals must take into account, 'the size and administrative resources of the employer's undertaking', and decide the issue, 'in accordance with equity and the substantial merits of the case'.[8] In practice reasonableness comes down to proper procedure, consistency and the appropriateness of dismissal as the form of disciplinary action to be taken. The last of these involves consideration of the severity of the employee's offence as well as any mitigating factors such as length of employment, good record, provocation and domestic or personal difficulties.

The onus of proof for establishing a fair reason lies with the employer. The employee, however, may wish to bring evidence and put arguments in order to challenge the reason put forward. On reasonableness the onus of proof is neutral. Both parties will need to present arguments and evidence on this point. If the act of dismissal itself is denied the employee will be responsible for establishing dismissal within the meaning of the Act. The employee will also be responsible for proof of loss for compensation purposes. If the dismissal is alleged to be on grounds of sex or race discrimination an employee with two years' continuous employment will be able to use unfair dismissal law where the onus of proof of the reason for dismissal is upon the employer. Those without the qualifying employment will be restricted to use of the discrimination legislation where the onus of proof is on the complainant. If the dismissal is alleged to be on union or non-union grounds the unfair dismissal legislation can be used irrespective of length of service: there is no qualifying employment. However, where the applicant has less than two years' continuous employment, the onus of proof of reason will lie with him or her rather than with the employer.

## Redundancy as a Reason for Dismissal

Because redundancy is one of the fair reasons for dismissal, a properly carried out dismissal by reason of redundancy will be a fair dismissal, although the employee, if qualified, may be entitled to a statutory redundancy payment. Properly carried out in this context means that the dismissal passes the general test of reasonableness, and in addition satisfies the selection requirements laid down in the statute (see below, pp. 96–8). The expiry of a fixed-term contract could be dismissal for redundancy if redundancy was the reason for non-renewal as it was in *Association of University Teachers* v. *University of Newcastle upon Tyne* where the funding for the course taught by the teacher had ceased.[9] This contrasts with the position in *North Yorkshire County Council* v. *Fay* where a teacher's fixed-term contract was not renewed when the post was filled on a permanent basis. This was a dismissal for 'some other substantial reason' rather than for redundancy. Expiry of an apprenticeship constitutes dismissal, but failure to appoint to a post will most likely be a fair dismissal for SOSR. Such a situation is not a redundancy and there is no obligation to offer a post (*North East Coast Shiprepairers Ltd* v. *Secretary of State for Employment*).

Redundancy is a management decision and unless there is bad faith or illegality it is unlikely to be susceptible to legal challenge. There cannot be any inquiry into the reasons for redundancy or into the rights and wrongs of it (*Moon and ors* v. *Homeworthy Furniture (Northern) Ltd*). However, in *Delanair Ltd* v. *Mead* the EAT stated that an employer must carry out an assessment of the needs of the business to see if it is practicable to perform the work with fewer employees, otherwise there would be no diminution in the requirement for employees (that is, no redundancy). This was in the context of reduced staffing for cost-saving reasons. In *Orr* v. *Vaughan* the EAT went further, holding that in making such an assessment the employer must act on 'reasonable information reasonably acquired'. More recently, in *James W. Cook & Co. (Wivenhoe) Ltd (in liquidation)* v. *Tipper and ors* the Court of Appeal stated that tribunals must not investigate the commercial and economic reasons for redundancy. However, they were entitled to examine whether the dismissal was genuinely on the grounds of redundancy and to require that the redundancy decision was based on proper information. In practice, the fact of needing fewer employees is what matters; once this has been established few tribunals will put the reasons under a microscope.

A change of employer within the meaning of the Transfer of Undertakings Regulations does not constitute dismissal; instead, continuity is preserved and terms and conditions are transferred. Where there is a dismissal for redundancy, either by transferor or transferee, and it arises out of the transfer, it would need to be justified on economic, technical or organizational grounds (see pp. 85–7).

## Selection for Redundancy

As already noted, a genuine redundancy properly carried out should not give rise to a claim let alone a finding of unfair dismissal. However, various aspects of the handling of redundancy are covered by the legislation and employers do from time to time fall foul of them. The main area which gives rise to problems is selection.

Selection must not be because of the employee's proposed or actual union membership or activities; because of proposed or actual union non-membership; in contravention of a customary arrangement; or in contravention of an agreed procedure. If the selection fails on any of these points the dismissal is automatically unfair, and the stage two test of reasonableness is not applied.[10] An employer has no defence to selection on grounds of unionism or non-unionism, once established, but may argue that there are 'special reasons' justifying a departure from a customary arrangement or agreed procedure.[11] In practice, employers will have to substantiate any arguments they put forward for special reasons by, for example, reference to the needs of the business. Something stronger than the reasonable employer defence will be needed (*Cross International* v. *Reid and ors*). Employees, on the other hand, will need to provide evidence to establish that there is an agreed procedure or customary arrangement, and that the employer has departed from it.

The provisions on automatically unfair selection are brought into play where the circumstances constituting the redundancy apply equally to two or more employees, one of whom is not made redundant. That is, there must be at least two candidates, one of whom is *not* chosen. The relevant unit is the undertaking and the employees must hold similar positions. Different grades or classes are not likely to be similar positions (*Robinson* v. *Carrickfergus Borough Council*; *Power and Villiers* v. *A. Clarke & Co.*).

Agreed procedures normally will apply only in unionized workplaces. The provisions have been held to apply to procedures collectively agreed with workers' representatives rather than to those agreed individually with an employee (*International Paint Co. Ltd* v. *Cameron*). A redundancy agreement can be implied from one party's acquiescence (*Henry* v. *Ellerman City Liners Ltd*). Customary arrangements are thought to apply to the undertaking rather than, say, the industry.[12] Voluntary redundancy was not a customary arrangement in *Rogers and ors* v. *Vosper Thorneycroft (UK) Ltd* because it merely threw up a pool of people from whom selection had to be made, rather than determining who would be selected. Conforming to an agreed procedure or customary arrangement does not make dismissal for redundancy automatically fair (*Evans and anor* v. *AB Electronic Components Ltd*). The general test of reasonableness must be satisfied and there is the possibility of an agreed procedure or customary arrangement being unreasonable. A customary arrangement failed the test in *N.C. Watling Ltd* v. *Richardson* because it gave insufficient weight to length of employment – the employers were not entitled to put their contracts into watertight compartments when selecting. In *Graham* v. *ABF Ltd* the selection criteria under an agreed procedure were not specific enough.

The law of unfair dismissal provides that the dismissal of a woman on grounds of pregnancy is automatically unfair, but it does not provide that selection for redundancy on such grounds is automatically unfair. However, the House of Lords decided in *Brown* v. *Stockton on Tees Borough Council* that the selection of a woman for redundancy because she was pregnant did constitute an automatically unfair dismissal. Employers must disregard the inconvenience of having to grant maternity leave. The Trade Union Reform and Employment Rights Act amends the legislation to make this clear and removes the requirement for a qualifying period of employment.

The final category of automatically unfair dismissal for redundancy is trades union reasons. Selection of shop stewards for redundancy because the employers believed (on the basis of the stewards' past activities) that they would engage in disruptive activities in the future was dismissal for redundancy on the grounds of trades union activities. It was held that the dismissals were automatically unfair (*Port of London Authority* v. *Payne and ors*).[13] Where redundancy is argued but is not the principal reason for the dismissals, the finding is likely to be dismissal on trades union grounds. This happened where 20 people were made redundant in a situation where there was a need for 13 fewer people, in order to include seven union members in the redundancy. The company then recruited seven replacements (*Controlled Demolition Group Ltd* v. *Lane and Knowles*). Where dismissal is on trades union grounds the two-year qualifying period of employment does not apply and nor does the NRA limit.[14] However, both of these apply where the dismissal is for redundancy and the *selection* is on trades union grounds, although the Trade Union Reform and Employment Rights Act (TURERA) now disapplies them.

Other than in the automatically unfair sorts of selection mentioned above, reasonableness must be judged,[15] including the selection criteria (*Bessenden Properties Ltd* v. *Corness*). If a redundancy is not reasonable it becomes an unfair dismissal. The general test is that the employer's selection must fall within a band of reasonable responses (see below, p. 104). It will be unreasonable only if no reasonable management would have made that selection (*N.C. Watling*; *BL Cars Ltd* v. *Lewis*). Thus, the criteria must not be vague (*Graham* v. *ABF Ltd*). Preference may be given to the disabled so that they are not made redundant but the general test of reasonableness still must be applied (*Seymour* v. *British Airways Board*). In any case, a registered disabled person may not be dismissed without reasonable cause if this would result in a company employing over 20 people being below the 3 per cent quota.[16] There is unlikely to be unfair selection if some employees are kept on by a liquidator to achieve an orderly winding-up of the company while the rest of the workforce are made redundant (*Fox Brothers (Clothes) Ltd* v. *Bryant*).

Care must be taken to avoid indirect sex discrimination. This is where a requirement or condition is applied which is such that the proportion of one sex which can comply with it is considerably smaller than the proportion of the other. For example, selecting temporary staff for redundancy might amount to indirect sex discrimination if these employees are predominantly female. Selecting part-timers almost certainly will since the vast majority of part-time employees are women. In *Clarke* v. *Eley (IMI) Kynoch Ltd* the dismissal of part-time employees was held to be unlawful sex discrimination and unfair dismissal. The unfair dismissal finding was because the employer's selection failed the reasonableness test.

Another issue is whether the application of the LIFO principle can amount to indirect sex discrimination, especially in areas to which women have gained access only in recent years. The EAT rejected such claims in *Brook and ors* v. *London Borough of Haringey*; LIFO was justified by a common sense need for length of service to be taken into account. The EAT commented that 'length of service is an essential ingredient in any redundancy selection, save in the most exceptional cases'. Thus, length of service as a selection criterion was assumed to be justifiable notwithstanding its indirectly discriminatory effect. The EAT also rejected claims that the exclusion of some largely male areas from the redundancy exercise was unlawful indirect discrimination since these areas were open to recruitment from both men and women.

More generally, the application of LIFO should be based on continuous rather than accumulated service – the latter might include breaks in employment (*International Paint Co. Ltd* v. *Cameron*). Whatever the criteria for selection, however, there should be a proper analysis of the available information, so that it is clear how, by whom and upon what basis the selection was made (*Bristol Channel Ship Repairers Ltd* v. *O'Keefe and ors*; *Greig* v. *MacAlpine*).[17] But it would be imposing too great a burden on employers to require them to prove that the information on which they made their selection was accurate – employers need establish the fairness of selection only in general terms (*Buchanan* v. *Tilcon Ltd*).

Last in, first out (LIFO) has been a widely-used criterion for redundancy selection for a number of reasons. It is least likely to result in worker resentment, conflict with trades unions and unfair dismissal claims. It enables experienced workers to be retained and so helps to maintain stability. It is also relatively cheap, because younger, shorter-serving employees are made redundant. Finally, it lends itself to a flexible approach, because it can be tempered by managerial interest criteria or applied only to particular parts of the workforce. Nevertheless, many employers see LIFO as too blunt an instrument, leaving them with minimal control over who goes and offering them little chance of ensuring that the best people stay. Some feel that it also adds to pay pressures, since most employees know that they are safe from redundancy and consequently are prepared to push for wage increases even though some jobs might be lost.

It is not surprising in the more competitive conditions of recent years that in selecting people for compulsory redundancy there has been a move away from the principle of last in, first out towards systems which give greater weight to the skills and experience which need to be retained in order to maintain an effective and balanced workforce.[18] The criteria used include:

- skills and/or qualifications, including experience and training;
- length of employment (seniority);
- standard of work performance including abilities, aptitude, adaptability and reliability;
- attendance record;
- disciplinary record;
- personal and/or domestic circumstances, such as ill-health;
- age;
- disaffection, due to, for example, poor promotion prospects.

Where redundancy is voluntary, criteria adopted have included, additionally, seniority (but first in, first out) and date of volunteering.

It will be important for management to have accurate information where, for example, absence or disciplinary records are being used as criteria. Management should know and take account of the reasons for absences (*Paine and anor* v. *Grundy (Teddington) Ltd*). The criteria must be reasonable and not in breach of any statute (for example, by being discriminatory on grounds of sex). They must also be applied reasonably, that is in a consistent and careful manner as between employees, again without breach of any statutory provisions.

Overall, some recognition of length of employment is likely to be regarded as reasonable, but so too would be its tempering with business requirements such as the need to keep employees with particular skills, good records, flexible attitudes and so on. Tribunals will want to identify the candidates for redundancy and to know the criteria used for selection between them. They will also want to know how the selection was operated, and by whom. In general, they will look for an objective approach, which includes taking into account length of employment.

Employers may find that performance appraisal schemes provide a useful structure for establishing fair and objective selection criteria and that the use of appraisal data can help to ensure that the act of selection is not itself unfair. Aspects such as skills and qualifications, standards of work, aptitude and attendance and disciplinary record may be considered alongside the traditional factor of length of employment. Alternatively, employers may wish to devise a special, separate performance assessment for redundancy selection purposes. This would have the advantage of not putting at risk the dialogue and development which is supposed to be part of a regular appraisal system. Moreover, where appropriate, the assessment criteria could be different. If such an approach is administered fairly it should protect an employer from a tribunal finding of unfair dismissal for redundancy. Above all, an employer must be able to defend the criteria chosen and the manner of application.

Management may feel it is worthwhile to provide a system of appeal against redundancy selection, although a failure to do this will not in itself make a redundancy dismissal unfair (*Robinson and ors* v. *Ulster Carpet Mills Ltd*).[19] In a unionized setting this might be a joint committee of management and union. In non-union situations, an appeal might lie to management at a more senior level. The right of appeal would be available to any individual selected for redundancy. Experience suggests that providing in-house opportunities for aggrieved employees in this way reduces the risk of claims being made to industrial tribunals.

The above analysis shows that such claims may be made on three bases. An employee may be able to mount two separate unfair dismissal challenges to the employer's selection decision, one on specific grounds (for example, breach of an agreed procedure), the other on the basis of unreasonableness (for example, the criteria adopted). In addition, a case of unfair selection on grounds of race or sex will be possible under the Race Relations Act 1976 or the Sex Discrimination Act 1975. The TURERA provides that selection for redundancy on health and safety grounds shall be automatically unfair and that no qualifying period of employment shall apply to employees exercising their rights in this area. Health and safety grounds include carrying out or proposing to carry out duties as a union safety representative, leaving a place of work if dangerous and carrying out duties as a member of a safety committee.

## Reasonableness

### *Aspects other than selection*

The reasonableness factor extends beyond selection to any other relevant issues. A main one in practice is lack of consultation. If redundancy becomes necessary 'the employer will normally not act reasonably unless he warns and consults with any employees affected, or their representative' (*Polkey* v. *A.E. Dayton (Services) Ltd*). The drift of the rulings in this and other cases is that consultation is required in the ordinary, normal case.[20] The logic is that consultation is necessary so that an attempt can be made to see if the needs of the business can be met without the dismissal and if not, whether the position of the employee can be improved. However, a failure to consult does not render an otherwise fair redundancy automatically unfair – the ultimate test is reasonableness. If a tribunal concludes that the employer reasonably took the view at the time of dismissal that the exceptional circumstances of the case would make consultation futile, it can find reasonableness even in the absence of proper procedure (*Polkey*; see, for example, *Spink* v. *Express Foods Group Ltd*).

The size and administrative resources of the undertaking may affect the nature or formality of the consultation process but cannot excuse the lack of any consultation at all (*De Grasse* v. *Stockwell Tools Ltd*). Consultation with the individual still may be required even where there is negotiation with a union. The individual employee may not know about the content of negotiations prior to a settlement (*Huddersfield Parcels Ltd* v. *Sykes*). Failure to consult a recognized union as required by the Trade Union and Labour Relations (Consolidation) Act 1992 (TULR(C)A) (see pp. 111–19) will not in itself make a dismissal for redundancy unfair (*Atkinson* v. *George Lindsay & Co.*; see also: *Hough* v. *Leyland DAF Ltd*) but it can be included as part of the reasonableness test.

An employer should take into account all relevant circumstances, not just those directly relating to or surrounding his grounds for dismissal (*Vokes Ltd* v. *Bear*). Thus, it would be unreasonable not to consider alternative work where there is a possibility. An employer should do what he reasonably can to seek alternative work (*Thomas and Betts Manufacturing Ltd* v. *Harding*) but if the company is part of a group he is not obliged *by law* to look for job opportunities elsewhere in the group (*MDH Ltd* v. *Sussex*). Ultimately there is no obligation to provide alternative work (*Merseyside and North Wales Electricity Board* v. *Taylor*). An employer's behaviour is not likely to be reasonable if the alternative work is not genuine (*Oakley* v. *The Labour Party*) or is offered on unreasonable terms (*Elliott* v. *Richard Stump Ltd*). Dismissal for refusal to accept alternative work on unreasonable terms is likely to be unfair. The principle decided in the early cases – before the onus of proof of reasonableness was taken off the employer and made neutral – remains valid: a reasonable employer will see if he can offer other employment as an alternative to redundancy (*Barratt Construction Ltd* v. *Dalrhymple*). The fact that an employer requires applications for alternative work rather than offering it (in the context of a reorganization) may not be unreasonable (*Rennie* v. *Grampian Regional Council* – where an offer had already been made but was rejected as unsuitable).

Next there is the special case of an employer's refusal to take a woman back after maternity leave, where the reason for the refusal is redundancy. The woman must be offered an alternative job if the employer, his successor or any associated employer has a suitable vacancy. The alternative work must be 'suitable in relation to the employee and appropriate for her to do in the circumstances'. The terms and conditions must not be substantially less favourable to her than those under her original contract.[21] Where there is a suitable vacancy which is denied to the woman, she will have been dismissed and the dismissal will be automatically unfair.[22] Indeed, in *John Menzies GB Ltd* v. *Porter* the EAT held the dismissal to be automatically unfair because the employers did not give proper consideration to the search for alternative employment. Where there is no suitable vacancy, there will be a dismissal for redundancy. Where the employer and any associated employer have five or fewer employees and there is no suitable vacancy, there will be no dismissal for the purposes of unfair dismissal law but there will be a dismissal for redundancy for RP purposes.[23]

### The general test

The general test of reasonableness in relation to unfair dismissal claims is 'how a reasonable employer in those circumstances in that line of business would have behaved' (*N.C. Watling*). However, employers will respond in different ways to a particular set of facts; thus, there will be a range of reasonable responses.[24] An employer's response will be reasonable if it falls within this range. Unreasonable means that no reasonable employer would have responded in that way. In the context of redundancy, dismissal will not normally be reasonable unless there has been advance warning, consultation with employees and/or their representatives, fair selection and reasonable steps to avoid or minimize redundancy (*Polkey*). In 1982 the EAT laid down some guidelines in *Williams and ors* v. *Compair Maxam Ltd*:

- An employer should give as much warning of impending redundancies as possible.
- There should be consultation with trades unions to ensure fairness and a minimum of hardship. Employers should seek to agree selection criteria with unions and to check that selection has been carried out according to the criteria.
- As far as possible the factors used in selection should be objective rather than subjective, for example, attendance record; job performance; experience; and length of service.
- There should be fair selection in accordance with the criteria and consideration of any union representations over selection.
- An employer should seek alternative employment instead of redundancy.

An employer should depart from the above only where there is a good reason.

This case was decided at a time when the EAT's prescriptive role was at its high point and, as is often the case, guidelines came to be taken as requirements. Subsequent decisions of the EAT put the matter in perspective, although the *Compair Maxam* principles remain good practice and are relevant to the question of reasonableness. Nevertheless, the absence of one or more of them will not necessarily lead to a finding of unfair dismissal; it will depend upon the circumstances of the case (*Grundy (Teddington) Ltd* v. *Plummer and Salt*; *Rolls Royce Motors Ltd* v. *Dewhurst and ors*). Also, the principles need to be applied with caution where the size and administrative resources of the employer are minimal (*Meikle* v. *McPhail (Charleston Arms)*). In fact, they are likely to be applicable mainly, perhaps only, in the context of substantial redundancies and where there is an independent, recognized trades union (*A. Simpson and Son (Motors)* v. *Reid and Findlater*).

There is no code of practice governing redundancy, the 1972 Industrial Relations Code of Practice having been revoked in 1991. The main procedural requirement of the code had been that management should, in consultation with employee representatives, seek to avoid redundancies. The code stated that where redundancy proved necessary, various matters should be considered, including the following:

- use of voluntary redundancy,[25] retirement and transfer;
- the phasing of the rundown of employment; and
- offers of help to employees in finding work with other employers.

It remains to be seen whether, in the absence of the code, industrial tribunals will find any of these matters to be relevant to the question of reasonableness when determining claims in relation to unfair dismissal for redundancy.

## The effect of a procedural slip-up

For many years industrial tribunals, when faced with an employer who had failed on some point of procedure (for example, a failure to consult the employee) applied what came to be known as the any difference test (*British United Shoe Machinery Co. Ltd* v. *Clarke*). They asked whether, if the employer had adopted the correct procedure it would have affected the outcome: would it have made any difference? Often the answer arrived at was no and many tribunals concluded on this basis that the dismissal was therefore fair, despite the statutory test being one of reasonableness. The position was changed fundamentally in 1987 by the ruling of the House of Lords in *Polkey* v. *A.E. Dayton (Services) Ltd*. Here it was held that the previous approach was wrong. The correct test was reasonableness, and the any difference test had no part to play in this.

However, while the any difference test could not be applied to the question of whether or not the dismissal was fair, it could be applied perfectly properly to the issue of compensation. Therefore, the chances that a redundancy would have occurred even if proper procedure had been followed can be reflected in what has come to be known as a *Polkey* reduction in the compensation. If a redundancy would merely have been delayed (for example, because of consultation) the compensation may be restricted to the period of delay. *Polkey* requires a tribunal to ask whether, if proper procedure had been followed, there would have been an offer of continued employment. If so, what would that employment have been and what wage would have been payable (*Red Bank Manufacturing Co. Ltd* v. *Meadows*)? A percentage reduction should be applied to the compensation to reflect the chance that the applicant would have been dismissed even if the procedure had been correct – that is, dismissed fairly and without compensation (*Rao* v. *Civil Aviation Authority*).

This chapter has sought to identify procedures in relation to the employee which will constitute good practice and should reduce the likelihood of unfair dismissal claims. In chapter 8 certain other procedural matters are highlighted, including the requirement to consult with independent, recognized trades unions.[26]

## Notes

1  EP(C)A, s. 90(1).
2  EP(C)A, s. 55(4).
3  SDA 1986, s. 3.
4  EP(C)A, s. 140(2)(e).
5  EP(C)A, schedule 13.
6  EP(C)A, s. 153.
7  EP(C)A, schedule 9, para. 2(1).
8  EP(C)A, s. 57(3).
9  Since there was a redundancy there was a breach of what is now TULR(C)A, s. 188(1) because there had been no consultation with the recognized trades union.
10  TULR(C)A, ss. 152–3 and EP(C)A, s. 59.
11  EP(C)A, s. 59
12  See Grunfeld, C., *The Law of Redundancy*, 3rd edition, London: Sweet & Maxwell, 1989, p. 308.

13   Under what is now TULR(C)A. The dismissal was on grounds of trades union activities as defined in s. 152(1) and therefore was held to be automatically unfair under s. 153

14   Also, interim relief may be available under TULR(C)A, s. 161. This is not the case where there is selection for redundancy on trades union grounds.

15   EP(C)A, s. 57(3).

16   Disabled Persons (Employment) Act 1944.

17   These cases were decided when the onus of proof of reasonableness lay upon the employer. The onus of proof is now neutral. As a matter of good practice, an employer should explain the selection process to his employees and ensure that managers and supervisors have been instructed and trained in the selection method. After all, they are the people applying it.

18   ACAS, *Redundancy Arrangements*, Occasional Paper 37, London: Advisory, Conciliation and Arbitration Service, 1987 (see p. 25). However, the need for employers to take care is underlined by the potential cost of employees taking unfair dismissal claims *as a group*. For example, it is reported that Hoover in South Wales settled 151 simultaneous individual claims which in aggregate cost £500,000 before any legal charges. An earlier case involving 36 port workers lasted over two years and cost in excess of £1 million (*Financial Times*, 6 January 1993).

19   There seems to be no reason why a serious defect in redundancy procedure (for example, in the application of the selection criteria), which could make a dismissal unfair, cannot be remedied by a proper application of the procedure on appeal. This follows the general unfair dismissal principle set out by the Court of Appeal in *Sartor* v. *P & O European Ferries (Felixstowe) Ltd.*

20   See, for example, *Freud* v. *Bentalls Ltd*; *Kelly* v. *Upholstery and Cabinet Works (Amesbury) Ltd*; *Holden* v. *Bradville Ltd*; *Ferguson and anor* v. *Prestwick Circuits Ltd*. The last-mentioned raises the question of whether employees *want* to be consulted. In a redundancy some three years earlier, the employers went through a consultation exercise only to be informed by the workforce that they would have preferred to have been told about their redundancy on the day that they were being made redundant. Therefore, in a second redundancy, the firm dispensed with consultation. This was not sufficient reason for failing to consult and in any case there was no evidence that the applicants had waived any right to consultation. 'Good industrial practice and the law require that, wherever possible, employees should be consulted before being dismissed on grounds of redundancy'. The Industrial Relations Code of Practice 1972, which required consultation save in exceptional circumstances (at para. 44) was revoked in 1991. In its absence tribunals may still regard consultation as part of the concept of reasonableness.

21 EP(C)A, s. 45(4).

22 EP(C)A. There is a dismissal by virtue of s. 56 and it is automatically unfair as a result of the operation of schedule 2, para. 2.

23 EP(C)A. This is because the definition of dismissal for RP purposes in s. 83 is different from that in ss. 55, 56 and 56A for unfair dismissal purposes (s. 56A prevents there being a dismissal).

24 This stems from the case of *British Leyland UK Ltd* v. *Swift*. See also: *Iceland Frozen Foods Ltd* v. *Jones*. For further details see: Towers, B., (Ed.), *A Handbook of Industrial Relations Practice*, 3rd edition, London: Kogan Page, 1992, pp. 348–9.

25 It will be rare for there to be an unfair dismissal for redundancy where redundancy has been voluntary (*Tocher* v. *General Motors (Scotland) Ltd*).

26 On the question of redundancy procedures generally, see ACAS: *Redundancy Handling*, Advisory Booklet No. 12, London: Advisory, Conciliation and Arbitration Service, 1988.

# 8
# Consultation with Trades Unions

---

Where a trades union is recognized by an employer, there are procedural requirements on the collective as well as the individual front. A failure to meet the requirements can prove expensive, since remedies are expressed in terms of an employee's pay and a substantial number of employees may be involved. Furthermore, the Secretary of State for Employment must be informed when ten or more redundancies are proposed and a failure here is a criminal offence. Before examining the above matters, however, this chapter considers individual employee rights in respect of written reasons for dismissal, notice and time off. Later, attention is given to outplacement and other forms of assistance.

## Written Reasons, Notice and Time Off

### Written statement of reasons for dismissal

This right is given to those who had two years' or more continuous employment with their employer prior to termination.[1] In the context of redundancy it is probably likely to be relevant only where the real or principal reason for dismissal is disputed. The right is triggered by the employee's request, (orally or in writing), so there can be no infringement without the employee having first made a request. A complaint can be made only if there has been an unreasonable refusal to comply with a request or if particulars of reasons were inadequate or untrue.

The claim for compensation for refusal to give written reasons is usually put on the same application form as the unfair dismissal claim itself, and must be at the Central Office of Industrial Tribunals within three months. The respondent employer has 14 days in which to reply to any request for written reasons. Where there is an unreasonable refusal to comply, or where the particulars of reasons were inadequate or untrue, a tribunal will make a penalty award of two weeks' pay. The two weeks' pay is gross, and since the right to have written reasons is separate from the right not to be unfairly dismissed there is no percentage deduction for any contributory fault. The award will usually be made at the end of the hearing of the substantive unfair dismissal claim. (The TURERA (s. 49(2) and sch. 8) substitutes 'failure' for 'refusal' in these provisions.)

## Notice periods

The EP(C)A lays down minimum notice periods.[2] The right is given to those employees with one month or more of continuous employment, and is as follows:

- if the continuous employment is less than two years – one week's notice
- one week's notice per year of continuous employment from two years to 12.

The minimum legal notice to be given where length of employment exceeds 12 years is still 12 weeks. The minimum notice which has to be given by the employee to the employer is one week. This does not increase with length of employment. Contractual arrangements may add to the statutory minimum on either side. Thus, the notice period can be in excess of the statutory minimum by agreement. For example, everyone being made redundant could be given three months' notice. However, it needs to be made clear that where there is pay in lieu, and it does not vary between individuals as would normally be the case, it is in fact pay in lieu rather than part of the RP.[3]

Fixed-term contracts of one month or less will attract the legal minimum notice only if the employee has already worked continuously for three months. Task contracts expected to last three months or less will be excluded unless there is already more than three months' continuous employment. Notice may be waived or payment in lieu accepted.[4] The right to terminate without notice because of the other party's repudiation is not affected. The employer must pay the employee during the notice period even if the employee is incapable of work because of sickness or injury or if there is no work, providing, in the latter case, that the employee is 'ready and willing to work'. Also, the employee must be paid if absent on holiday 'in accordance with the terms of his employment relating to holidays'.[5]

For infringement of notice rights the remedy is to sue through the courts for wrongful dismissal, that is, dismissal not in accordance with the terms of the contract. In this respect pay in lieu of notice is regarded as damages for breach of contract (*Delaney* v. *Staples (T/A De Montfort Recruitment)*). However, there soon may be implementation of statutory provision for industrial tribunals to hear certain breach of contract cases: the TURERA contains provisions in this area. The notice rights apply to those fixed-term contracts with provision for termination by notice within the fixed term, but do not apply to Crown servants.

Under common law there can be an agreement for withdrawal of the notice or an agreement to defer it (see *Mowlem (Northern) Ltd* v. *Watson*). Where employees stay back to assist in an orderly rundown of plant, it is common for employers to make retention payments.

### *Time off to look for work or to arrange training*

An employee given notice of dismissal by reason of redundancy is entitled to a reasonable amount of paid time off before the expiry of his notice.[6] The time off is within working hours in order to look for new employment or make arrangements for training for future employment. There is a two-year qualifying period for this right, as a result of which the hours qualification applies (see p. 92). The right to paid time off is not affected by the fact that an employee may not be eligible for a statutory RP (*Dutton* v. *Hawker Siddeley Aviation Ltd*).[7] An employee refused time off or pay for time off may complain to an industrial tribunal within three months. The maximum compensation payable is two-fifths of a week's pay. The amount of paid time off can be extended beyond this in practice, for example, to one week.[8] It should be noted that the two-fifths of a week's pay is *not* subject to the statutory limit.

## Consultation with Trades Unions

When employers are proposing to dismiss one or more employees by reason of redundancy, they must consult with the representatives of any independent trades union that they recognize.[9] The available defence is that special circumstances have made it not reasonably practicable to consult, but in such cases employers still must take all steps that *are* reasonably practicable. The employees covered by these provisions are not required to have any periods of qualifying employment, nor any continuous employment at all (so that the number of hours worked is not relevant). However, some employees are excluded: Crown employees; House of Commons staff; merchant seamen (but the TURERA provides for their inclusion); share fishermen; employees ordinarily working outside Great Britain; employees working under contracts for three months or less or task contracts expected to last for three months or less, unless in both cases they have already worked for more than three months; those employed in the police service.[10] There still will be a right to consultation in cases where the employee is not entitled to a statutory RP. Union representatives must be consulted about the proposed redundancy of an employee even if he is not a union member, as long as he is of the description of employees for which the union is recognized (*National Association of Teachers in Further and Higher Education* v. *Manchester City Council*).

A trades union is an organization of workers whose principal purposes include regulating the relations between those workers and employers or employers' associations. The definition includes federations of unions.[11] Independent means that a union is not under the domination or control of an employer and is not liable to interference by an employer tending towards such control. A union may apply to the Certification Officer for a certificate of independence.[12] Recognition[13] means that a trades union is accepted by an employer (or associated employers) for the purposes of collective bargaining, that is, for the purposes of negotiations related to or connected with:

a  terms and conditions of employment, or the physical conditions in which any workers are required to work,
b  engagement or non-engagement, or termination or suspension of employment or the duties of employment, of one or more workers,
c  allocation of work or the duties of employment as between workers or groups of workers,
d  matters of discipline,
e  the membership or non-membership of a trades union on the part of a worker,
f  facilities for officials of trades unions, and
g  machinery for negotiation or consultation, and other procedures, relating to any of the foregoing matters, including the recognition by employers

or employers' associations of the right of a trades union to represent workers in any such negotiation or consultation or in the carrying out of such procedures.[14]

A collective agreement is an agreement between union(s) and employer(s) on one or more of these matters.[15] In this context, the term 'associated employers' does not refer to membership of an employers' association. Rather, it refers to employers where one is a company controlled by the other, or where both are companies controlled by some third person.[16]

The case law confirms that recognition means direct recognition by the employer. It is not sufficient that the employer is a member of an employers' association which recognizes various unions on an industry-wide basis (*National Union of Gold, Silver and Allied Trades* v. *Albury Bros*; see also *Cleveland County Council* v. *Springett*). Representation of an employee by a full-time union official in respect of a disciplinary matter is not recognition for bargaining purposes (*Transport and General Workers' Union* v. *Courtenham Products Ltd*) nor is the granting of general representational (as opposed to bargaining) rights (*Union of Shop, Distributive and Allied Workers* v. *Sketchley Ltd*). Presumably the same is true where a union is afforded consultation rights. There must be an express or implied agreement to recognize, and if implied, there must be clear and unequivocal conduct consistent with recognition (*National Union of Tailors and Garment Workers* v. *Charles Ingram Co. Ltd*). Stating on an official form (such as that used for notifying proposed redundancies to the Secretary of State) that a union is recognized would be strong evidence. Recognition can be partial, that is, granted in respect of some issues but not others; but if it is limited to certain grades of employees or locations, the consultation rights will be similarly limited. The onus of proof appears to lie with the trades union to demonstrate the existence of a recognition agreement (*Transport and General Workers' Union* v. *Andrew Dyer*). It is of no relevance that recognition was forced upon an employer by the employees taking industrial action.

The right to be consulted is given to the 'trades union representative', which means 'an official or other person authorized by the trades union to carry on collective bargaining with that employer'.[17] If the Act is to apply, the employer actually must be proposing redundancy rather than just considering it. Proposing means that an employer is at least somewhere near making a decision to dismiss.

That is, the stage should have been reached where a specific proposal has been formulated (*Hough* v. *Leyland DAF Ltd*). This means that the employer should have a view as to numbers, timing and manner of execution (*Association of Patternmakers and Allied Craftsmen* v. *Kirvin Ltd*). There is a presumption that redundancy is the reason for the dismissal (or proposed dismissal) unless the contrary is shown.[18] Where redundancies are not proposed, but occur as a result of a court winding-up order, there will be no duty to consult (*In re Hartlebury Printers Ltd and ors (in liquidation)*).

Consultation rights extend to non-unionists of the same description as the members represented by the union. Consultation must begin 'at the earliest opportunity'.[19] More specifically:

- where the employer proposes to make redundant 100 or more employees at one establishment within 90 days or less the consultation must start at least 90 days before the first dismissal;
- where the number is 10 employees or more in one establishment within 30 days or less it must start at least 30 days before the first dismissal.

Establishment is not defined in the legislation and has to be determined on the facts of each case. In *Barratt Developments (Bradford) Ltd* v. *Union of Construction, Allied Trades and Technicians*, the EAT held that 14 building sites administered from one head office were a single establishment. It seems that the degree of management control, the extent of geographical separation and perhaps the permanence or otherwise of the operation may be relevant factors. However, establishment relates to the employer proposing to dismiss. Where several employing companies operate on the same site, and are owned by a holding company, there is no question of treating them as one establishment because they are separate employers (*E. Green and Son (Castings) Ltd and ors* v. *Association of Scientific, Technical and Managerial Staffs and Amalgamated Union of Engineering Workers*).

There is no specified minimum length of time by which consultation must begin in cases involving fewer than ten employees. The fact that 28 days is specified in relation to the protective award in such cases does not imply that this is necessarily the appropriate period for consultation (*James Longley Ltd* v. *Union of Construction, Allied Trades and Technicians*). Proposing to dismiss means intending to give notice of termination or to dismiss without notice. Since an employer proposing to dismiss must consult, it follows that there must be some consultation before notice of dismissal is given (*National Union of Teachers* v. *Avon County Council*). Consultation must start before the proposed date of the first dismissal (*E. Green and Son; Transport and General Workers' Union* v. *Ledbury Preserves (1928) Ltd*). As a matter of good practice, consultation should start before any public announcement of the redundancies. There must be 'sufficient meaningful consultation' before dismissal notices are sent out in order to give the union representatives time to consider properly the proposals being put to them (*Ledbury*). In another case, an industrial tribunal held that there should be sufficient information to allow the union representatives to make constructive proposals (*General and Municipal Workers' Union (Managerial, Administrative and Technical Staffs Association)* v. *British Uralite Ltd*).

The legislation does not define what is meant by consultation although it does state that an employer must consider and reply to any representations by the trades union representatives, giving reasons if any are rejected. There is no statutory requirement to accept any particular representation, but an employer making up his mind in advance might be taken as not having considered that representation. Information must be provided for the purpose of consultation. An employer must disclose in writing to trades union representatives the whole of the following:

a   the reason for his proposals;
b   the numbers and descriptions of employees whom he proposes to dismiss;
c   the total numbers of employees of such description(s) employed at that establishment;
d   the proposed method of selection; and
e   the proposed method of carrying out the dismissals, having regard to any agreed procedure, and the period over which they are to take effect.[20]

Whether, and at what stage, sufficient information has been provided for consultation to begin is a matter of fact for the industrial tribunal. Sufficient may not mean that *all* the information listed above has been given; and tribunals should state reasons where they consider the information is not sufficient (*GEC Ferranti Defence Systems Ltd* v. *Manufacturing Science and Finance Union*).

Consultation does not require that the employees to be made redundant are named (*Spillers-French (Holdings) Ltd* v. *Union of Shop, Distributive and Allied Workers*), but an employer must provide more detail about the proposed method of selection than a statement indicating that it will be 'determined in consultation with union representatives' (*E. Green and Son*). Industrial tribunals have also said that employers should disclose information necessary to show how severance pay is calculated and the TURERA makes this a statutory requirement.[21]

Employers as a matter of good practice may consult, or negotiate, in respect of other matters, such as:

- earnings and other money issues (for example, relocation expenses) where there is redeployment;
- the basis of selection (for example, department or company);
- whether employees may leave before their notice expires without losing entitlement to their RP;
- extension of the length of trial periods for redeployment;
- retention of company benefits after redundancy;
- provisions to avoid the redundancy of apprentices and other trainees; and
- time off in excess of that required by the legislation.

An employer may argue that there were 'special circumstances' for failing to comply with one or more of the statutory provisions, viz: the time requirements (effectively an advance warning of redundancy), the written information requirements and the obligation to consider and reply to any representations. Tribunals will generally ask: what are the 'circumstances'? are they 'special'? did they make full consultation not 'reasonably practicable'? and did the employer do as much as was 'reasonably practicable'? Special means 'exceptional or out of the ordinary' (*Bakers' Union* v. *Clark's of Hove Ltd*). Therefore, insolvency does not of itself constitute special circumstances (*Clark's of Hove*). Nor do the dismissal of workers to make an insolvent company more attractive to buyers, and the subsequent closure of the company: these are common occurrences (*General, Municipal and Boilermakers' Union* v. *Messrs Rankin and Harrison (as Joint Administrative Receivers of Lawtex plc and Lawtex Babywear Ltd)*). In contrast, the sudden withdrawal of credit facilities and the appointment of a receiver by a bank were special circumstances (*Union of Shop, Distributive and Allied Workers* v. *Leancut Bacon Ltd*). Once the special circumstances defence is established, it will be unjust for a tribunal to make an adverse declaration (*Clark's of Hove*).

A recognized, independent trades union, but not a trades union representative or an employee, may make a complaint to an industrial tribunal no later than three months after the dismissal takes effect that one or more of the statutory requirements has not been met. An employer arguing special circumstances will have the burden of proof upon him on this point. The tribunal, if it finds an infringement of the statute, must make a declaration to that effect, and may also make a 'protective award'. This is an award that the employer shall pay the employee remuneration for a protected period. The award does not name individual employees; rather, it specifies the description of employees to which it relates (*Spillers-French*).

The period is at the discretion of the tribunal, but must not exceed 90 days in the 100 or more employees case, 30 days in the 10 or more employees case, and 28 days in any other case. The test is what is 'just and equitable . . . having regard to the seriousness of the employer's default'.[22]

What is just and equitable is a matter for the industrial tribunal (*Sovereign Distribution Services Ltd* v. *Transport and General Workers' Union*). The protective award compensates for loss arising out of the lack of consultation but is also punitive because the tribunal must have regard to the seriousness of the employer's breach (*Spillers-French*). Such a breach may not be considered very serious if it comprises nothing more than a failure to put in writing information which was given orally, as in *Association of Scientific, Technical and Managerial Staffs* v. *Hawker Siddeley Aviation Ltd*. A failure to give reasons for the redundancies, or a failure to provide information on one of the other matters listed in (a)–(e) on p. 15 might be viewed more seriously (*Transport and General Workers' Union* v. *Nationwide Haulage Ltd*). A failure to consult at all (as in *Clark's of Hove*) or consultation undertaken only at the last minute (as in *E. Green and Son*) might be even more serious.

The financial significance of these awards can be considerable because there are often substantial numbers of employees covered by them. As an example, an industrial tribunal in Edinburgh was reported as recently making a protective award of 48 days' pay against GEC Defence Systems. This was thought to amount to somewhere between £600,000 and £800,000. The award may be reduced by any contractual payments made in respect of the protected period, including damages for breach of contract. Conversely, the award can be set off against any contractual liabilities. (The TURERA repeals both these provisions.) The award runs from the date of the first dismissal or the date of the award if that is earlier. Date of the first dismissal means when the first of the proposed dismissals was expected to take effect (*E. Green and Son*; *Transport and General*

*Workers' Union* v. *Ledbury Preserves (1928) Ltd (No. 2)*). The protective award does not extend the employee's employment for the purpose of calculating a statutory RP or for the purpose of the qualifying period for a statutory RP. Where the employer is insolvent, up to eight weeks' pay from any protective award (subject to the maximum weekly limit) is payable from the National Insurance Fund.[23]

An employee will lose the right to a protective award if while still employed he unreasonably terminates his contract of employment or is fairly dismissed for a reason other than redundancy. An unreasonable refusal of suitable alternative work will lose the employee the protective award for that part of the protected period during which he would otherwise have been employed. If the employee accepts the offer there is a trial period during which reasonable termination by the employee preserves entitlement to the protective award.[24]

An employee whose employer fails to pay him during the protected period may apply to a tribunal within three months of the last day of non-payment. A tribunal may order an employer to pay. In practice, therefore, those employers who fail to consult and pay a protective award are simply buying out the union's right to consultation.

The statutory requirements may be adapted, modified or excluded if there is a collective agreement which is 'on the whole at least as favourable' as the legislation, but there must be provision for independent resolution of disputed matters.[25] The statutory requirements may be adapted, modified or excluded only upon the application of all the parties to the collective agreement to the Secretary of State and by order of the Secretary of State. However, employers are free to use the statutory provisions as a minimum. They may offer consultation beyond the requirements of the law, for example, by consulting over longer periods, by consulting with organizations other than recognized trades unions (for example, staff bodies which are not independent, recognized unions) and by consulting over a range of matters which is wider than that specified in the legislation.

Where there is a change of employer falling under the Transfer Regulations there will be no redundancy as a result of the transfer itself but the consultation requirements of the regulations will apply. The provisions described above will operate where the transferor or the transferee is proposing to make an employee redundant. Union recognition and any redundancy agreements are likely to be transferred to the transferee.

The European Community has recently adopted a directive to strengthen employees' rights where there is a collective redundancy (see p. 175). The requirements of this directive, and some unmet requirements of the 1975 directive, are contained in the Trade Union Reform and Employment Rights Act. Where a redundancy decision is made by someone who controls the employer (for example, a parent company in another EC state or outside the EC) and the employer is not provided with information about the redundancy, the employer will not be permitted to argue the special circumstances defence if there is a failure to consult or to notify the Secretary of State. The information requirements will be extended by the inclusion of the method for calculating extra-statutory RPs and there will be a wider definition of redundancy dismissals for redundancy consultation purposes. Redundancy will mean dismissal for a reason or reasons not related to the individual concerned. Consultation will have to be with a view to reaching agreement and will have to include the avoidance of redundancy, its minimization and the mitigation of its consequences. Pay in lieu will not be deductible from any protective award.

## Notification of Proposed Redundancies to the Secretary of State for Employment

An employer must notify the Secretary of State of proposed redundancies involving ten or more dismissals in accordance with certain time periods (see above, p. 114).[26] The unit for consideration is the establishment rather than the organization. Where redundancies have already been notified they do not count again if there are further redundancies requiring notification. Thus, 40 redundancies within 30 days (requiring notification 30 days before dismissal) followed by another 80 within 30 days (requiring 30 days' notification) do not become 120 requiring 90 days' notification. Compliance with the notification process does not prevent an employer from altering his plans (for example, abandoning the implementation of redundancies or postponing them) if circumstances change. Failure to comply leaves the employer liable to a fine.[27] Copies of the notification must be sent by the employer to representatives of independent trades unions which organize any of the categories of workers to be made redundant but the duty to notify the Secretary of State arises even in the absence of a recognized, independent trades union.[28]

The notice to the Secretary of State must 'be in such form and contain such particulars . . . as the Secretary of State may direct'.[29] Where consultation with trades union representatives is required the notice must identify the union concerned and specify the date when consultation started. The Secretary of State can by written notice require further information.[30] The Department of Employment encourages use of a standard form for notification. A copy of this is included below (figure 5). An employer may plead 'special circumstances' as a defence if there has not been notification, but must do all that is reasonably practicable to comply with the requirement to notify.

## Outplacement and Other Aspects

The management of redundancy may be improved by adopting one or more of a number of other procedural devices. None of these are required by law, but they may make redundancy less difficult to achieve and may, by creating an image of social responsibility, reward the firm in the longer run. One such device would be to phase any rundown so that the effects on the local community are felt more gradually and time given for alternative employment strategies to develop.

Where opportunities for employment exist elsewhere in the firm, that is, at other locations, an employer might provide details of such vacancies to those whose jobs are disappearing. These people might undergo assessment to determine suitability for other jobs, and where thought suitable there might be trial periods before any permanent relocation. To be successful, redeployment policy is likely to need to have resources and to be ongoing. This is because attention needs to be devoted to housing, family, social and community considerations as well as to maintenance of earnings and seniority. Employees will need visits for inspection purposes in advance of moving, and there may be substantial retraining costs. It is not surprising that prominent examples of this sort of policy have been large-scale relocations over a relatively long period of time with the advantage of public finance, as in the coal and steel industries.

If there are few or no opportunities for redeployment, an employer may be able to offer help by means of a number of labour market initiatives. An employer may be able to determine the retraining needs of those being made redundant (in respect of outside jobs),

Employment Department                    Employment Protection Act 1975, Section 100

# Advance notification of redundancies

**What is this all about?**

As an employer, you are required by law to notify proposed redundancies of ten or more employees.

**When do I have to do that?**

If 10 to 99 employees might be dismissed as redundant from one establishment over a period of 30 days or less -
**you must give at least 30 days' notice.**

If 100 or more employees might be dismissed as redundant from one establishment over a period of 90 days or less -
**you must give at least 90 days' notice.**

The date of notification is the date it is received by the Employment Department. For more details please see leaflet PL833 "Redundancy consultation and notifictaion". You can get one from any Jobcentre or Unemployment Benefit Office.

**What information do I have to give?**

It is the information requested in the form below. You can send a letter instead but you must give the information asked for in the form. Please send a separate notification for each establishment where it is proposed that ten or more employees will be made redundant.

**Where do I send the form or letter?**

You may have been given an addressed envelope for the return of the form. If so, please use it. If not, please return the form to the Employment Department, Redundancy Payments Office, Hagley House, 83-85 Hagley Road, Birmingham B16 8QG, or to the nearest Employment Department office.

**What if I notify you about redundancies and the circumstances change?**

The fact that you have notified us about redundancies does not commit you to them. But if the circumstances change, please let us know.

**Anything else?**

Yes. One or more group of workers to be made redundant may belong to a recognised independent trade union. If so, you must send a copy of your notification to the representatives of each such trade union.

**Data Protection Act 1984**

We will put the information you give us on to a computer. We will pass it to selected government agencies who may offer to help you deal with the proposed redundancy. Information will not be given to any non governmental agencies without your consent.

**These notes are for guidance only. They are not a full and authoritative statement of the law.**

- Where there are boxes offering a choice of answer, please tick those that apply.
- If there is not enough space for your reply, please continue on a seperate sheet of paper and attach it to this form.
- Use a separate form for each establishment where redundancies will occur.

1 Name of employer (**CAPITALS** please)

2 Address

Postcode

3 Telephone number

4 Who should we contact if we have any enqueries about this form?
Name (**CAPITALS** please)

5 Please give this person's business address and telephone number if either is not the same as given above:
Address

Postcode

6 Telephone number

7 What is the address of the establishment at which the employees are employed?
  - as given at 2 ☐     • as given at 5 ☐
or give details below:

8 What is the nature of the main business at that establishment?

9 Please tick one or more boxes to show the main reason(s) for the redundancies:
  - lower demand for products or services ☐ A
  - completion of all or part of contract ☐ B
  - transfer of activities to another workplace following a merger ☐ C
  - introduction of new technology ☐ D
  - introduction of new plant or machinery ☐ E
  - changes in work methods or organisation ☐ F*
  - transfer of activities to another workplace for other reasons ☐ G*
  - something else ☐ H*
                    * please give details below

HR 1 ————————————————————————————————— over ▶

**Figure 5**  Advance notification of redundancies          *Continued over*

and direct them towards training opportunities outside the firm. On occasions, employers have gone beyond this and actually provided advance training for those being made redundant so that they fare

**10** How many people do you currently employ at this establishment?

| | employees |

**11** How many employees at this establishment do you think **might** be made redundant?

| | employees |

**12** If you have the information available, please give figures below to show the numbers employed/to be made redundant:

| Occupational group | Number employed now | Number to be made redundant |
|---|---|---|
| **Manual** | | |
| • skilled | | |
| • semi-skilled | | |
| • unskilled | | |
| **Clerical** | | |
| **Managerial/ technical** | | |

**13** How many apprentices and long term trainees may be made redundant?

| | apprentices/trainees |

**14** How many employees under 20 years old (incuding apprentices and trainees) may be made redundant?

| | employees |

**15** Do you propose to close down the establishment?

Yes ☐        No ☐

**16** When will the first proposed redundancy take effect?

| Day | Month | Year |
|---|---|---|
| | | |

**17** When will the last proposed redundancy take effect?

| Day | Month | Year |
|---|---|---|
| | | |

**18** Briefly, how do you propose to choose which employees should be made redundant?

**Trade union involvement**

**19** Are any of the groups of employees who may be made redundant represented by a recognised trade union?

Yes ☐

No ☐ ▶ *go to 'Declaration' below*

**20** Please give below the name and address of each such trade union:

**21** When did consultation with the trade union(s) start?

| Day | Month | Year |
|---|---|---|
| | | |

**22** Has full agreement with the trade union(s) been reached?

Yes ☐ ▶ *please enclose a copy of the agreement or give brief details below:*

No ☐

**Declaration**

I certify that the information given on this form is, so far as I know, correct and complete.

Signed

Date

Position held

For our use

**Figure 5**　*Continued*

better in the labour market. Such training can include new skills, enhancement of existing skills and job search technique. The last-named may include occupational guidance, instruction on how to write job applications and presentation at interviews. The Department of Employment can be involved, sometimes on-site, to assist with job placement and the provision of information, for example, on training opportunities and relocation assistance.

Some employers have contacted other firms in their area with details of those searching for work, recognizing that many jobs are filled without there being a public advertisement or notice. More exceptionally, and in cases where redundancy has the potential for creating substantial damage to the local economy, employers have established agencies with a remit to attract new employment to the area. Coal and steel are again examples and of course a major consideration is the ability to offer financial inducements and managerial expertise to the incoming employers.[31] A further way in which an employer creating redundancies can enhance the labour market position of those being made redundant is to provide a recall facility. That is, the ex-employee is given first choice of any vacancies which may arise at a later date.

An employer may provide information and counselling with the aim of assisting the redundant employee in other ways. This might include counselling in respect of unemployment, financial information, such as in relation to entitlements (RPs, pensions, state benefits) or investment opportunities, and assistance to those intending to become self-employed. It is likely that there will be a substantial difference in post-redundancy experience between those who will be in receipt of an enhanced and early pension and those who will not. The counselling should reflect the expected experiences of different categories of employee, taking a longer-term as well as an immediate view. Those in the early retirement category are likely to have experiences which are on balance positive. They are more likely to find the financial position satisfactory, may enjoy having more time and, depending upon the previous work environment, may have improved health. Their counselling might cover, among other things, pension entitlement, investment of money, retirement planning and part-time employment. In the context of widespread unemployment, the middle-aged people may be the ones needing most help. They are the ones most likely to suffer as a result of redundancy. A combination of family responsibilities on the one hand and unemployment and lack of income on the other may add up to financial difficulties and a deterioration in health. Boredom and frustration may fuel the latter. The need for retraining is likely to be more important with this group because of their age, but it also will be a factor with younger people even though they are likely to be better placed in the labour market.

Finally, an interesting package has been put together by British Coal Enterprise (BCE). They provide on-site facilities for assisting redundant employees in respect of:

- coping with the idea of redundancy;
- preparing and circulating a CV;
- letters of application;
- completing application forms;
- effective job hunting;
- interview techniques;
- setting up a business;
- researching the job market;
- pre-retirement planning; and
- opportunities for retraining.[32]

Initially, in 1984, BCE were concerned solely with resettling employees made redundant by British Coal. Now, their services are on offer more generally. Almost three-quarters of *The Times* Top 500 companies use outplacement services in some form, and BCE claims to be the largest UK provider. A full BCE package comprises consultancy and a range of products (including books, videos and course notes) but the products can be bought without the consultancy. A typical BCE outplacement project would go through four stages:[33]

*1 Dealing with redundancy* This stage would include counselling to encourage a positive attitude, and awareness training so that the employee knows what services will be available.

*2 Defining potential* This stage would involve analysing and defining an individual's strengths, skills and aptitudes, and might include various assessments, for example, of career direction. A personal action plan would be prepared.

*3 Job seeking* Included at this stage would be training in methods of job search, and where appropriate, information about self-employment. Pre-retirement courses also would be available.

*4 Getting the job* The final stage would include training in, and information about: CV preparation, letter writing, interview techniques and self-presentation.

On completion of the programme, BCE would present the client with a full report.

From 6 April 1993, outplacement counselling provided by employers – either directly or via third parties – will be completely tax-exempt. Previously it was included as part of the RP package, tax-free up to £30,000 (see pp. 155–6).

*Notes*

1  Increased from six months by the Employment Act 1989, s. 15. The two years applies to any employment commencing on or after 26 February 1990 (Employment Act 1989 (Commencement and Transitional Provisions) Order, SI 1990/189).
2  EP(C)A, s. 49. For the purposes of notice, a week does not have to be a pay week as defined in s. 153(1) of EP(C)A.
3  A standard number of weeks' pay in lieu may be regarded as a redundancy payment if it bears no relation to and is not connected with the individual's notice rights (*Decision of the Social Security Commissioner*, 23 September 1986, case CU/364/1985).
4  EP(C)A, s. 49(3). These are not the same. It is submitted that there need be no payment in lieu where a party waives their right to notice since the other party is not in breach of contract by terminating without notice. The more common situation is where a payment is accepted instead of the notice. It seems that the waiving of notice rights applies only to contractual rights and does not apply to the qualifying right for a RP or for the purpose of calculating a RP. In such cases s. 90(3) of the EP(C)A would postpone the relevant date even if the employee accepted pay in lieu or waived his right to notice (*Staffordshire County Council* v. *Secretary of State for Employment*).
5  EP(C)A, schedule 3, para. 2 (in respect of employments for which there are normal working hours). The employee must be paid in such circumstances regardless of whether notice is given by the employer or the employee. However, this will not be the case where the notice which must be given by the employer is at least one week more than the statutory minimum, since this disapplies schedule 3.
6  EP(C)A, s. 31. The following are excluded: employees normally working outside Great Britain; merchant seamen; share fishermen; and members of the police service.
7  An employee might be ineligible for a RP but eligible for time off where an offer of suitable alternative employment is unreasonably refused. The right to paid time off is not qualified in this way.
8  Incomes Data Services, *Redundancy Terms*, Study 464, London: IDS, 1990 (see p. 6).

9   TULR(C)A, s. 188(1).

10  TULR(C)A, ss. 273, 278, 280, 282–5 and 295–6.

11  TULR(C)A, s. 1.

12  TULR(C)A, ss. 5–6; providing that it is listed. The Certification Office is part of the Department of Employment and is an independent statutory authority. The Certification Officer exercises functions specified in various statutes including the listing of trades unions. Being listed is evidence that an organization is a trades union. The process of listing is voluntary, but being listed is a prerequisite for obtaining a certificate of independence and tax relief for provident funds.

13  TULR(C)A, s. 178(3).

14  TULR(C)A, s. 178(2).

15  TULR(C)A, s. 178(1).

16  TULR(C)A, s. 297.

17  TULR(C)A, s. 196.

18  TULR(C)A, s. 195(3). This presumption applies also to the provisions requiring notification of proposed dismissals for redundancy to the Secretary of State.

19  TULR(C)A, s. 288(2).

20  These requirements are laid down in TULR(C)A, s. 188(4). The information, in writing, may be conveyed by personal delivery or by letter to a union-nominated address or the union's head office (s. 188(5)). A public body's failure to consult as required by statute may be subject to judicial review. British Coal's 1992 decision to avoid using the industry's colliery closure consultative procedure was held to be unlawful because it was in breach of the industry procedure and was irrational (*R* v. *British Coal Corporation and Secretary of State for Trade and Industry ex parte Vardy and ors*).

21  ACAS, *Employment Handbook*, London: Advisory, Conciliation and Arbitration Service, 1990 (see p. 73), TURERA, s. 34(2)(a).

22  TULR(C)A, s. 189(4)(b).

23  EP(C)A, s. 122.

24  TULR(C)A, s. 191.

25  TULR(C)A, s. 198.

26  TULR(C)A, s. 193. There is no requirement to notify where it is proposed to make redundant fewer than ten employees. The following are not subject to the notification requirement: Crown employees; House of Commons staff; merchant seamen; share fishermen; employees ordinarily working outside Great Britain; and employees on contracts for terms of three months or less, or on task contracts lasting for less than three months, unless, in both cases, there is already more than three months' continuous employment (TULR(C)A, ss. 278, 282–5 and 295–6). Those employed in the police service are not subject to

the notification requirement because they are expressly excluded from the definition of employee (TULR(C)A, s. 280).

27  The employer is liable on summary conviction to a fine not exceeding level five on the standard scale, currently £5,000 (TULR(C)A, s. 194(1) and Criminal Justice Act 1991, s. 17).

28  TULR(C)A, s. 193(6), but there appears to be no penalty if this is not done.

29  TULR(C)A, s. 193(4)(c).

30  TULR(C)A, s. 193(5).

31  See Jones, K., *The Human Face of Change*, London: Institute of Personnel Management, 1974.

32  IDS, *Redundancy Terms*, p. 8.

33  BCE Outplacement, *Customised Outplacement Programmes*, Mansfield: BCE Ltd, 1992.

# 9

# Redundancy Payments

---

## The Statutory Redundancy Payments Scheme

### *Eligibility*

An employee dismissed by reason of redundancy may be entitled to a statutory redundancy payment (RP). To qualify, the employee must have been continuously employed by the employer or an associated employer for two years or more,[1] be dismissed by reason of redundancy and be below the upper age limit. Where normal retiring age (NRA) does not discriminate on grounds of sex and is 65 years or lower, the NRA will be the limit. In any other circumstances 65 applies (see table 2).[2] The concept of NRA is explained above, see pp. 93–4.

**Table 2** Maximum age limit for entitlement to statutory redundancy payments

|                                         | *Eligibility limit (must be under)* |
|-----------------------------------------|:-----------------------------------:|
| Non-discriminatory NRA of 65 or below   | NRA                                 |
| Non-discriminatory NRA above 65         | 65                                  |
| No NRA at all                           | 65                                  |
| Discriminatory NRAs                     | 65                                  |

Since employment before the age of 18 years does not count towards computation of continuous employment, a person has to be at least 20 to obtain a payment.[3]

The following employees are excluded from the legislation:

a   Part-time workers without sufficient continuous employment (see above, p. 92).[4]
b   Share fishermen.[5]
c   Crown servants. These are covered by their own separate agreements.[6]
d   Employees whose contract requires them to ordinarily work outside Great Britain, unless they are working in Great Britain on the instructions of their employer[7] at the time of the redundancy. An employee who is outside Great Britain at the time of redundancy will be entitled to a RP only if he ordinarily works in Great Britain.[8]
e   Employees of foreign governments.[9]
f   Domestic servants who are close relatives of the employer.[10]

There are special provisions for former registered dock workers.[11] National Health Service employees and merchant seamen are no longer excluded.[12] The Secretary of State may make regulations to extend the statutory RP scheme to holders of public office who are not employed under a contract of employment.[13] There are also provisions bringing offshore workers within the statutory scheme.[14]

The scheme includes those on fixed-term contracts, excluding apprenticeships. Where the contract is for a term of two years or more there will be a right to claim a payment on expiry of the contract unless there has earlier been a written agreement to waive that right. It would then have to be decided whether the non-renewal was for reason of redundancy (see *Lee* v. *Nottinghamshire County Council*; *North Yorkshire County Council* v. *Fay*). The waiver applies only to the time of expiry and not to redundancy within the term of the contract, although there would be no entitlement to a RP unless the two-year qualifying period had already been met. The waiver may be made at any time before the fixed term expires, but lapses on expiry, although it can be renewed.[15]

It is possible that the exclusion of part-time employees from the RP scheme amounts to unlawful sex discrimination, because the vast majority of part-timers are women. However, the Court of Appeal has ruled that this discrimination is lawful, finding it to be objectively justified by virtue of its positive effect on the level of employment (*R* v. *Secretary of State for Employment ex parte Equal Opportunities Commission*).

### Meaning of dismissal and onus of proof

The onus is upon the employee to establish that there was a dismissal. Dismissal was defined in chapter 7 (p. 90).[16] Any notice must specify a date of termination or contain material from which a date is ascertainable. Otherwise, there will be no dismissal. Thus, an application for voluntary redundancy and the employer's agreement to release, but with the date to be decided, did not constitute dismissal (*Burton Group Ltd* v. *Smith*).

A fixed-term contract must have a date of expiry, and the expiry of such a contract is a dismissal. A contract which is to last as long as it takes to perform a particular task, without any fixed date of expiry, is not a fixed-term contract and the end of the contract does not constitute a dismissal (*Wiltshire County Council* v. *NATFHE and Guy*). The same is true of a contract, again not for a fixed period, which is determined by something other than performance. In the case of *Brown and ors* v. *Knowsley Borough Council* the contract was to last as long as outside finance remained available. When outside finance ceased, the contract ended, but it was not a dismissal.

There are also provisions to ensure that certain events which normally would not be treated as dismissal are so treated.[17] These are: death of a personal employer, dissolution of a partnership, the receivership and liquidation of a company and the frustration of the employment contract by any event affecting the employer. The dismissal will be taken to be by reason of redundancy if there is no renewal of contract or re-engagement under a new contract by the employer, any person to whom the power to dispose of the business has passed or any new owner of the business, providing that the reason for such non-renewal or non re-engagement is redundancy.[18]

Once the fact of dismissal is established the reason for the dismissal is to be taken as redundancy if not proved otherwise. This means the employer has to show that the reason was not redundancy. Where unfair dismissal is also alleged, the onus is upon the employer to show the reason for dismissal.

The concept of redundancy was analysed in chapter 5 (see pp. 71–3). It was noted that it involved a dismissal wholly or mainly due to: a cessation of the entire business; cessation in the particular place where the employee was employed; or a diminution in the requirement for employees to perform work of a particular kind (either generally or in the place where the employee was employed). The Court of Appeal has applied a contractual test to work of a particular kind so that it refers to work that the employee can be required to do under his contract of employment (*Nelson* v. *British Broadcasting Corporation*; *Haden Ltd* v. *Cowen*; applied by the EAT in *Pink* v. *White and White & Co. (Earls Barton) Ltd*). Similarly, place of work means the contractual place – wherever the employee can be required to work (*United Kingdom Atomic Energy Authority* v. *Claydon*; *Sutcliffe* v. *Hawker Siddeley Aviation Ltd*; *Rank Xerox Ltd* v. *Churchill and ors*). Thus, mobility clauses may be important in determining whether or not there is a redundancy. Such terms may be express or implied. They may be implied from collective agreements, custom in the firm or from the nature and practice of the work. In *O'Brien* v. *Associated Fire Alarms Ltd* the court implied a mobility term from the nature and practice of the work but held that it limited mobility to daily travelling distance from home or to within a reasonable distance from home.

## *Industrial action or misconduct by the employee*[19]

If before giving notice of redundancy the employer is entitled to dismiss for misconduct, a redundancy payment will not be payable even if the reason for dismissal is redundancy (*Simmons* v. *Hoover Ltd*). The test is a contractual one – whether the employee is in breach of contract such that dismissal is justified – rather than that of reasonableness, as found in unfair dismissal law (*Bonner* v. *H. Gilbert Ltd*). An employee will thus lose entitlement to a RP if dismissed for striking prior to his employer giving him the 'obligatory' notice, that is, that required by contract or statute (whichever greater). Where misconduct, other than taking part in a strike, occurs (or is discovered) during the 'obligatory' notice period, and the employer dismisses for that misconduct, the tribunal has discretion to award the whole of the RP or such part as it thinks fit. An employee will retain his right to a RP if dismissed for striking during the 'obligatory' notice period. An employee also will retain his right to a RP even if the redundancy was caused to some extent by earlier industrial action in which he took part. This might be the case, for example, where the action caused permanent loss of customers. Equity is not the principle to be applied, however (*Sanders* v. *Ernest A. Neale Ltd*).

## *Lay-offs and short-time working*

A redundancy payment may be made when an employee is laid off or put on short-time working.[20] A person is laid off for the purposes of the legislation where in any week the employer provides no work of the kind that the employee is employed to do, and under the contract of employment there is no entitlement to be paid. Short-time is where there is a diminution in the work provided which leads to at least a 50 per cent reduction in pay. Where the employer offers alternative work which is within the terms of the employee's contract and which would prevent the occurrence of short-time working, he shall be taken to have 'provided' the work even if it is refused by the employee (*Spinpress Ltd* v. *Turner*). In the case of both short-time working and lay-off there must be four consecutive weeks or six weeks in 13 (no more than three being consecutive). Weeks of lay-off or short-time caused by strikes or lock-outs anywhere cannot be counted. To claim a RP, the employee has to give notice of termination of employment and follow a rather complicated procedure.[21]

This involves the employee giving written notice to the employer of intention to claim a RP. Such notice must be given within four weeks of the last of the weeks of lay-off or short-time on which the claim is based, but must occur after the period of lay-off or short-time working relied on is complete (*Allinson* v. *Drew Simmons Engineering Ltd*). The employer then has seven days to serve a counter-notice stating that he will contest liability. An offer of alternative work will not constitute a valid counter-notice (*Reid* v. *Arthur Young and Son*). Where such a counter-notice is served, and not withdrawn, an employee will not be entitled to a RP unless he or she applies to an industrial tribunal and is successful. An employer's defence is that normal working is reasonably to be expected no later than four weeks after the date on which the employee serves notice of intention to claim, and that such working can reasonably be expected to last for at least 13 continuous weeks without there being a lay-off or short-time in any week. Normal working involves the employee being employed under the same contract as before (*Neepsend Steel and Tool Corporation* v. *Vaughan*). The defence is available only if a valid counter-notice has been served by the employer.

The employee must give whatever length of notice of termination of contract is required by the contract. Where the employer has not served a counter-notice, the employee's notice of termination must be within four weeks of his notice of intention to claim. Where there has been a counter-notice which has been withdrawn, notice of termination must be within three weeks of the withdrawal. Where the employer has not withdrawn his counter-notice and a RP has been awarded by an industrial tribunal, notice of termination must occur within three weeks of the employee being notified of the tribunal's decision.

The time limits in the above scheme cannot be extended. Therefore an employer may be able to defend a claim on the basis that the employee has failed to give one or both of the required notices within the allowed time. On the other hand, an employer may lose a case by not serving a counter-notice in time.

The lay-off or short-time must be lawful. Otherwise, if the employee is ready and willing to work, he is entitled to be paid and these provisions will not apply. Where lay-off or short-time working is in breach of contract, employees may succeed in claiming constructive dismissal by reason of redundancy and obtaining a RP by this route (*Powell Duffryn Wagon Co. Ltd and anor* v. *House and ors; Miller* v. *Hamworthy Engineering Ltd*). An employer will not be able to argue that the lay-off was caused by a strike if the case is pursued as a constructive dismissal. That argument relates only to the separate lay-off and short-time provisions (*R.H. and D.T. Edwards Ltd* v. *Evans and Walters*). Contractual guarantee pay of at least half a week's pay will remove entitlement to a RP under the lay-off and short-time provisions but statutory guarantee pay (see below, pp. 151–2) may not, since it is not remuneration under the contract.

## Alternative employment

An employee will not be entitled to a redundancy payment where the employer, an associated employer or, where a business changes hands, the new owner, offers 'suitable' alternative employment and the employee 'unreasonably' refuses it. An offer must be made before the expiry of the old contract and must take effect immediately on the ending of that contract or no later than four weeks afterwards. It would not be a valid offer under the legislation if it took effect *before* the ending of the old contract (*McHugh* v. *Hempsall Bulk Transport Ltd*). It need not be in writing.

Whether the employee will retain the right to a redundancy payment after refusing an employer's offer of alternative work (or terminating the contract during the trial period – see below) will depend on it being established that either the new employment was unsuitable, or that it was suitable but the employee was reasonable in refusing it. In the statute these two questions are to be decided separately, but in practice they become fused. Indeed, in *Spencer and Griffin* v. *Gloucestershire County Council* the Court of Appeal warned against too rigid a distinction between the two because some factors might be common to both. The onus is upon the employer to prove both suitability and unreasonableness (*Jones* v. *Aston Cabinet Co. Ltd*) and these are matters of fact for a tribunal to decide (*Standard Telephones and Cables Ltd* v. *Yates*, in respect of suitability).

Suitable means suitable 'in relation to the employee'.[22] In general it means 'substantially equivalent' (*Taylor* v. *Kent County Council*). Skills, earnings, nature of previous work, what is traditionally acceptable and geographical location have all been important.[23] In *Smith* v. *R. Briggs and Co. Ltd* a big drop in earnings potential made the work unsuitable. In the *Yates* case, alternative work as an assembly line operator was not sufficiently skilled and therefore was not suitable for someone who was a skilled craft worker. Lower status can also make alternative work unsuitable, as in *Harris* v. *E. Turner and Sons (Joinery) Ltd* in which an instructor was offered alternative work back on the shop floor. In *Taylor* v. *Kent County Council* a headmaster was offered alternative work in a mobile pool of teachers. This was unsuitable despite the fact that the previous level of pay was safeguarded. Sometimes a number of factors operate together – in *Jackson* v. *Harris Queensway plc* there was no proposal to compensate the employee for extra travelling time, his guaranteed wage was going to be reduced by a fifth and the job involved more responsibility. The EAT held that such alternative employment was not suitable.

Whether it is reasonable for the employee to refuse suitable alternative employment has often been a matter of the employee's personal or domestic circumstances, although job-related factors also can be relevant. Thus, in *Tocher* v. *General Motors (Scotland) Ltd* it was reasonable to refuse alternative employment which involved a drop in both pay *and* status. In *Morganite Crucible Ltd* v. *Street* it was unreasonable to refuse a temporary job which would last 12–18 months, but it might be reasonable to refuse something likely to last for a very short period. In *Spencer and Griffin*, alternative cleaning work at a lower standard of cleanliness was suitable, since it is for the employer to determine standards, but the employees' refusal to accept the work on the ground that they did not wish to work at the lower standard was reasonable. Significant extra travel time and/or cost is another factor which may make a refusal reasonable.[24]

Where an employee accepts renewal of contract or re-engagement under a new contract, there will have been no dismissal.[25] An offer of re-engagement will need to have been made before the expiry of the old contract but this is not the case where the contract is renewed (confirmed by the EAT in *SI (Systems and Instruments) Ltd* v. *Grist and Riley*). An offer must take effect immediately on the ending of the old contract or no later than four weeks afterwards. Again, the offer need not be in writing, but it will need to conform to the general requirements of the law of contract, viz: the offer must be sufficiently certain and unconditional, and it must be communicated to the employee. If there is to be renewal or re-engagement, the employee must accept it without qualification. Continuity is preserved for statutory purposes.[26] Where the terms of the new employment differ from those of the old there is a requirement for a 'trial period' of four weeks to establish whether the employment is suitable, without loss of entitlement to claim the RP. Four weeks means four calendar weeks, so that if the period includes a shut-down of work the employee will have less than four weeks to try out the new employment (*Benton* v. *Sanderson Kayser Ltd*). The statutory trial period can be extended by agreement but only for the purpose of retraining (confirmed by the EAT in *Meek* v. *J. Allen Rubber Ltd and Secretary of State for Employment*). Any such agreement must be in writing, must specify the end of the trial period and the terms and conditions which will apply afterwards, and be made before the employee starts work under the new contract. There can be more than one statutory trial period where an employer makes a further offer of alternative employment.

A common law trial period occurs where new terms are imposed by an employer in the context of a redundancy and in breach of contract, but the employer does not dismiss and the employee neither resigns (claiming constructive dismissal) nor accepts the new terms (*Air Canada Ltd* v. *Lee*). The trial period will be of a reasonable length, but can be a specific period by agreement. The common law trial period stems from the general contractual rule that a party to whom an offer is made should have the opportunity to appraise the terms of the offer. Once the employee has had a reasonable length of time to appraise the new terms, the old contract ends, the new one begins and the statutory trial period commences (*Turvey and ors* v. *C.W. Cheyney & Son Ltd*). Therefore, the statutory trial period follows any contractual trial period, but there is a problem with this. Presumably the new contract will begin only if and when the employee accepts the new terms, but if this happens there will not have been a dismissal to bring into play the statutory trial period. None of the above prevents contractual trial periods of a longer duration (for example six weeks, 13 weeks and so on) but these would not preserve the statutory right to a RP unless the statutory requirements were met (that is, the purpose would have to be retraining, the agreement would have to be in writing and so on). However, they would preserve the contractual right to a RP if this had been agreed.

Where there is a change in the ownership of a business, and a new owner agrees to continue the employment of the employee on the same or mutually agreed new terms, the provision for suitable alternative employment and a trial period apply as if it was still the original employer. The Transfer of Undertakings Regulations 1981 may also apply[27] (see pp. 79–81).

### Continuity of employment

Continuous employment was defined in chapter 7 (see pp. 92–3). Employment is assumed to be continuous unless proved to the contrary. Thus the onus here is on the employer. Continuous employment ends on the 'relevant date'. Where there is notice it is the date of expiry of notice. Where there is no notice it is the date of termination. Where it is the expiry of a fixed-term contract, it is the date of expiry of the contract. The trial period delays the relevant date only for the purposes of calculating the time available for making a claim. For RP purposes, employment before the age of 18 years does not count when computing the length of continuous employment.

Continuous employment for statutory RP calculation purposes excludes any service which has counted for a previous statutory RP[28] (confirmed by the EAT in *Rowan* v. *Machinery Installations (South Wales) Ltd*). However, the previous service will be included if the employer was not liable to make that earlier payment (for example, because the operation of the Transfer Regulations meant that there was no dismissal) (*Gardener* v. *Haydn Davies Catering Equipment (1988) Ltd (in liquidation) and ABE Catering Equipment Ltd*). This is because the earlier payment was not a statutory RP. Continuous employment will be reduced by the payment of a statutory RP only for statutory RP purposes. This was confirmed by the EAT in *Hempell* v. *W.H. Smith & Sons Ltd* where an employee was re-engaged by her former employer in a new job after being dismissed for redundancy and receiving a RP. She was dismissed a second time, shortly afterwards, on the ground that she was unsuitable. Her continuity for the purposes of an unfair dismissal claim included the period prior to the first dismissal.

Once an employee has become qualified for a RP he or she will remain so until becoming employed under a contract for less than eight hours a week *and* in any week actually being employed for fewer than 16 hours.[29]

A strike does not interrupt continuity of employment, but the week in which a strike takes place does not count for the purpose of reckoning service.[30] During periods in which there is no contract of employment there is no break in continuity if there is sickness or injury lasting up to 26 weeks and these weeks also count. There is no break if there is a temporary cessation of work, absence by arrangement or custom, or because of pregnancy or confinement, and again, the weeks count.

For RP purposes, movement between local government employers does not break continuity of employment.[31]

### Computation of payment

The payment is calculated on the basis of age, length of employment and earnings according to the formula in table 3.[32] The Department of Employment produces a ready reckoner for RPs which is included on pp. 138–9. There are no current proposals to standardize RPs throughout the EC or to lay down a minimum level. No employment beyond 20 years is counted, so the maximum payment is $20 \times 1\frac{1}{2} =$ 30 weeks' pay. There is a maximum level of weekly pay which is counted, currently £205.[33] The maximum statutory RP is therefore £6,150. The earnings limit is reviewed annually as required by the EP(C)A.[34] As the age of 65 is approached, payments are reduced by one twelfth for each complete month over 64.[35]

**Table 3** Formula for computation of redundancy payments

| Age | Number of weeks' pay per year of employment in the particular age category |
|---|---|
| Under 22 years | $\frac{1}{2}$ |
| 22–40 | 1 |
| 41 and over | $1\frac{1}{2}$ |

**Table 4** DE ready reckoner for redundancy payments

| Age (years) \ Service (years) | 2 | 3 | 4 | 5 | 6 | 7 | 8 | 9 | 10 | 11 | 12 | 13 | 14 | 15 | 16 | 17 | 18 | 19 | 20 |
|---|---|---|---|---|---|---|---|---|---|---|---|---|---|---|---|---|---|---|---|
| 20 | 1 | 1 | 1 | 1 | — | | | | | | | | | | | | | | |
| 21 | 1 | 1½ | 1½ | 1½ | 1½ | — | | | | | | | | | | | | | |
| 22 | 1 | 1½ | 2 | 2 | 2 | 2 | — | | | | | | | | | | | | |
| 23 | 1½ | 2 | 2½ | 3 | 3 | 3 | 3 | — | | | | | | | | | | | |
| 24 | 2 | 2½ | 3 | 3½ | 4 | 4 | 4 | 4 | — | | | | | | | | | | |
| 25 | 2 | 3 | 3½ | 4 | 4½ | 5 | 5 | 5 | 5 | — | | | | | | | | | |
| 26 | 2 | 3 | 4 | 4½ | 5 | 5½ | 6 | 6 | 6 | 6 | — | | | | | | | | |
| 27 | 2 | 3 | 4 | 5 | 5½ | 6 | 6½ | 7 | 7 | 7 | 7 | — | | | | | | | |
| 28 | 2 | 3 | 4 | 5 | 6 | 6½ | 7 | 7½ | 8 | 8 | 8 | 8 | — | | | | | | |
| 29 | 2 | 3 | 4 | 5 | 6 | 7 | 7½ | 8 | 8½ | 9 | 9 | 9 | 9 | — | | | | | |
| 30 | 2 | 3 | 4 | 5 | 6 | 7 | 8 | 8½ | 9 | 9½ | 10 | 10 | 10 | 10 | — | | | | |
| 31 | 2 | 3 | 4 | 5 | 6 | 7 | 8 | 9 | 9½ | 10 | 10½ | 11 | 11 | 11 | 11 | — | | | |
| 32 | 2 | 3 | 4 | 5 | 6 | 7 | 8 | 9 | 10 | 10½ | 11 | 11½ | 12 | 12 | 12 | 12 | — | | |
| 33 | 2 | 3 | 4 | 5 | 6 | 7 | 8 | 9 | 10 | 11 | 11½ | 12 | 12½ | 13 | 13 | 13 | 13 | — | |
| 34 | 2 | 3 | 4 | 5 | 6 | 7 | 8 | 9 | 10 | 11 | 12 | 12½ | 13 | 13½ | 14 | 14 | 14 | 14 | — |
| 35 | 2 | 3 | 4 | 5 | 6 | 7 | 8 | 9 | 10 | 11 | 12 | 13 | 13½ | 14 | 14½ | 15 | 15 | 15 | 15 |
| 36 | 2 | 3 | 4 | 5 | 6 | 7 | 8 | 9 | 10 | 11 | 12 | 13 | 14 | 14½ | 15 | 15½ | 16 | 16 | 16 |
| 37 | 2 | 3 | 4 | 5 | 6 | 7 | 8 | 9 | 10 | 11 | 12 | 13 | 14 | 15 | 15½ | 16 | 16½ | 17 | 17 |
| 38 | 2 | 3 | 4 | 5 | 6 | 7 | 8 | 9 | 10 | 11 | 12 | 13 | 14 | 15 | 16 | 16½ | 17 | 17½ | 18 |
| 39 | 2 | 3 | 4 | 5 | 6 | 7 | 8 | 9 | 10 | 11 | 12 | 13 | 14 | 15 | 16 | 17 | 17½ | 18 | 18½ |
| 40 | 2 | 3 | 4 | 5 | 6 | 7 | 8 | 9 | 10 | 11 | 12 | 13 | 14 | 15 | 16 | 17 | 18 | 18½ | 19 |
| 41 | 2 | 3 | 4 | 5 | 6 | 7 | 8 | 9 | 10 | 11 | 12 | 13 | 14 | 15 | 16 | 17 | 18 | 19 | 19½ |
| 42 | 2½ | 3½ | 4½ | 5½ | 6½ | 7½ | 8½ | 9½ | 10½ | 11½ | 12½ | 13½ | 14½ | 15½ | 16½ | 17½ | 18½ | 19½ | 20½ |

| | | | | | | | | | | | | | | | | | | | | |
|---|---|---|---|---|---|---|---|---|---|---|---|---|---|---|---|---|---|---|---|---|
| 43 | 3 | 4 | 5 | 6 | 7 | 8 | 9 | 10 | 11 | 12 | 13 | 14 | 15 | 16 | 17 | 18 | 19 | 20 | 21 |
| 44 | 3 | 4½ | 5½ | 6½ | 7½ | 8½ | 9½ | 10½ | 11½ | 12½ | 13½ | 14½ | 15½ | 16½ | 17½ | 18½ | 19½ | 20½ | 21½ |
| 45 | 3 | 4½ | 6 | 7 | 8 | 9 | 10 | 11 | 12 | 13 | 14 | 15 | 16 | 17 | 18 | 19 | 20 | 21 | 22 |
| 46 | 3 | 4½ | 6 | 7½ | 8½ | 9½ | 10½ | 11½ | 12½ | 13½ | 14½ | 15½ | 16½ | 17½ | 18½ | 19½ | 20½ | 21½ | 22½ |
| 47 | 3 | 4½ | 6 | 7½ | 9 | 10 | 11 | 12 | 13 | 14 | 15 | 16 | 17 | 18 | 19 | 20 | 21 | 22 | 23 |
| 48 | 3 | 4½ | 6 | 7½ | 9 | 10½ | 11½ | 12½ | 13½ | 14½ | 15½ | 16½ | 17½ | 18½ | 19½ | 20½ | 21½ | 22½ | 23½ |
| 49 | 3 | 4½ | 6 | 7½ | 9 | 10½ | 12 | 13 | 14 | 15 | 16 | 17 | 18 | 19 | 20 | 21 | 22 | 23 | 24 |
| 50 | 3 | 4½ | 6 | 7½ | 9 | 10½ | 12 | 13½ | 14½ | 15½ | 16½ | 17½ | 18½ | 19½ | 20½ | 21½ | 22½ | 23½ | 24½ |
| 51 | 3 | 4½ | 6 | 7½ | 9 | 10½ | 12 | 13½ | 15 | 16 | 17 | 18 | 19 | 20 | 21 | 22 | 23 | 24 | 25 |
| 52 | 3 | 4½ | 6 | 7½ | 9 | 10½ | 12 | 13½ | 15 | 16½ | 17½ | 18½ | 19½ | 20½ | 21½ | 22½ | 23½ | 24½ | 25½ |
| 53 | 3 | 4½ | 6 | 7½ | 9 | 10½ | 12 | 13½ | 15 | 16½ | 18 | 19 | 20 | 21 | 22 | 23 | 24 | 25 | 26 |
| 54 | 3 | 4½ | 6 | 7½ | 9 | 10½ | 12 | 13½ | 15 | 16½ | 18 | 19½ | 20½ | 21½ | 22½ | 23½ | 24½ | 25½ | 26½ |
| 55 | 3 | 4½ | 6 | 7½ | 9 | 10½ | 12 | 13½ | 15 | 16½ | 18 | 19½ | 21 | 22 | 23 | 24 | 25 | 26 | 27 |
| 56 | 3 | 4½ | 6 | 7½ | 9 | 10½ | 12 | 13½ | 15 | 16½ | 18 | 19½ | 21 | 22½ | 23½ | 24½ | 25½ | 26½ | 27½ |
| 57 | 3 | 4½ | 6 | 7½ | 9 | 10½ | 12 | 13½ | 15 | 16½ | 18 | 19½ | 21 | 22½ | 24 | 25 | 25 | 27 | 28 |
| 58 | 3 | 4½ | 6 | 7½ | 9 | 10½ | 12 | 13½ | 15 | 16½ | 18 | 19½ | 21 | 22½ | 24 | 25½ | 25½ | 27½ | 28½ |
| 59 | 3 | 4½ | 6 | 7½ | 9 | 10½ | 12 | 13½ | 15 | 16½ | 18 | 19½ | 21 | 22½ | 24 | 25½ | 27 | 28 | 29 |
| 60 | 3 | 4½ | 6 | 7½ | 9 | 10½ | 12 | 13½ | 15 | 16½ | 18 | 19½ | 21 | 22½ | 24 | 25½ | 27 | 28½ | 29½ |
| 61 | 3 | 4½ | 6 | 7½ | 9 | 10½ | 12 | 13½ | 15 | 16½ | 18 | 19½ | 21 | 22½ | 24 | 25½ | 27 | 28½ | 30 |
| 62 | 3 | 4½ | 6 | 7½ | 9 | 10½ | 12 | 13½ | 15 | 16½ | 18 | 19½ | 21 | 22½ | 24 | 25½ | 27 | 28½ | 30 |
| 63 | 3 | 4½ | 6 | 7½ | 9 | 10½ | 12 | 13½ | 15 | 16½ | 18 | 19½ | 21 | 22½ | 24 | 25½ | 27 | 28½ | 30 |
| 64 | 3 | 4½ | 6 | 7½ | 9 | 10½ | 12 | 13½ | 15 | 16½ | 18 | 19½ | 21 | 22½ | 24 | 25½ | 27 | 28½ | 30 |

*Note*: Read off employee's age and number of complete years' service. Service before the employee reached the age of 18 does not count. The table will then show how many weeks' pay the employee is entitled to. For the definition of a week's pay, see below, pp. 140–2. The redundancy payment due is to be reduced by one twelfth for every complete month by which the age exceeds 64 years. Entitlement ceases entirely at 65 or at normal retiring age if below 65 and non-discriminatory.

The statutory scheme lays down minimum RPs. Payments must not be below the level provided by the scheme, but may be added to voluntarily. However, the right to make enhanced RPs sometimes may be circumscribed. A district auditor has successfully challenged the authority of local government to make RPs in excess of the amount provided for by statute, although the relevant statute – regulations under the Superannuation Act 1972 – allows payments in excess of those under the EP(C)A by removing the limit on weekly earnings.[36] It also places an upper limit on payments and the employers exceeded this (*R* v. *North Tyneside Metropolitan Borough Council ex parte Allsop*).

Rules for calculating a week's pay are laid down in Schedule 14 of the EP(C)A. The date on which pay is ascertained – the calculation date – is when the minimum statutory notice was due, or where there was notice less than the statutory minimum, or no notice, when the contract of employment ended.[37] A week's pay for those whose pay does not vary with the amount of work done will be the pay received for working normal weekly hours. The concept of normal weekly hours is not defined but where there is entitlement to overtime pay it will be the number of hours beyond which overtime becomes payable. Where there is contractual overtime normal weekly hours will include it. Otherwise, overtime pay will not count for RP purposes (*Tarmac Roadstone Holdings Ltd* v. *Peacock and ors*).[38] Where pay does vary with the amount of work done, hourly pay is averaged over 12 weeks and the result multiplied by normal weekly hours. If there is shift working so that pay varies from week to week according to shift pattern, the total number of hours over 12 weeks is divided by 12 and the result multiplied by average hourly pay. If there are no normal weekly hours a week's pay will be weekly remuneration averaged over 12 weeks.

The treatment of overtime will depend upon the type of case. As noted, where pay does not vary with the amount of work done, overtime is to be excluded unless it is contractual. Where pay varies with the amount of work done or from week to week because of shift patterns, overtime hours are to be included in the calculation of average hourly pay but stripped of the overtime premium. This can give rise to anomalies where an incentive bonus does not increase with overtime working because the effect of working overtime is to reduce hourly pay (*British Coal Corporation* v. *Cheesbrough*). The example in table 5 illustrates the point.

**Table 5** Inclusion of overtime in the calculation of average hourly pay for redundancy payments purposes

| | Bonus (£) | Pay at £4 per hr (£) | Total pay (£) | Total hours (hours) | Average hourly pay (£) |
|---|---|---|---|---|---|
| Normal weekly hours (40) | 40 | 160 | 200 | 40 | 5.00 |
| Normal weekly hours plus 10 hours' overtime | 40 | 200 | 240 | 50 | 4.80 |

Remuneration means money paid by the employer under the contract of employment for work done by the employee.[39] It includes all contractual payments by an employer and is gross (*Secretary of State for Employment* v. *John Woodrow and Sons (Builders) Ltd*), but does not extend to payments in kind. Thus, company cars, free meals and free accommodation will not form part of 'a week's pay', although a deduction from pay in respect of such an item might be a basis on which it could be included. Expenses will not form part of pay (because they are not a payment for work done) unless there is an element of profit for the employee (for example, mileage expenses paid at something in excess of the expense actually incurred). In tax law, anything beyond the true expense is taxable income (*Perrons* v. *Spackman (HM Inspector of Taxes)*) and if the employer and employee have agreed to treat taxable income as untaxed expenses in order to reduce the amount of tax paid, the contract of employment will be void for illegality and no RP will be payable. Courts and tribunals will investigate this issue where the evidence points to it even if it is not part of the pleadings. Tips and gratuities will not form part of pay since these are not a payment by the employer. However, the proceeds from a service charge upon customers, which were paid by an employer to his employees, were held to form part of pay (*Tsoukka and ors* v. *Potomac Restaurants Ltd*). Discounts on the company's products, cheap loans and so on are excluded because they do not represent a payment for work done. Pay will not include an *ex gratia* Christmas bonus. By the same token, production bonuses and commission will form part of pay if they are contractual. Contractual guarantee pay will not be remuneration because it is not a payment for work done by the employee, but a payment for being on call probably will be. Allowances for working in abnormal conditions may be included. Such an allowance – for working in excessive heat – was included when a tribunal calculated the average remuneration of shiftworkers in *Randell* v. *Vosper Shiprepairers Ltd*.

An employer must give an employee a written statement indicating how the amount of any statutory RP has been calculated.[40] If an employer fails to comply 'without reasonable excuse' he will be guilty of an offence and liable on summary conviction to a fine not exceeding level one on the standard scale (currently £200). In such circumstances the employee may by notice in writing require the statement from the employer within a period specified in the notice. The period must be no less than one week. If the employer fails to comply with the notice (again, 'without reasonable excuse') there will be a further offence and liability on summary conviction to pay a fine not exceeding level three on the standard scale (currently £1,000). If an offence is committed by a corporate body with the 'consent or connivance of', or is 'attributable to any neglect on the part of, any director, manager, secretary or similar officer', he as well as the corporate body shall be guilty and liable to prosecution.[41]

## Applications to industrial tribunals

If the payment is not agreed and made, the employee who wishes to claim must make a complaint to an industrial tribunal or an application in writing to the employer. If neither of these is done within six months the application is time-barred unless an unfair dismissal application has been made to a tribunal. However, a tribunal can still award a payment if a claim is made within the following six months if it is 'just and equitable' to do so. An application is made to a tribunal when it is received at the tribunal office rather than when it is posted (*Secretary of State for Employment* v. *Banks and ors*) but if the applicant has already written to the employer making a claim, and this was done within the time limit, he may apply to a tribunal at any time thereafter. Where a tribunal hears a claim from a Crown servant under a contractual scheme, the time limit will be as laid down in the contractual scheme, or if no limit is stated, six years[42] (*Greenwich Health Authority* v. *Skinner*). Where an employee wishes to claim unfair dismissal for redundancy as well as for payment of a RP, the tribunal application in respect of unfair dismissal will need to be made within three months. A woman who received a lower RP than a man under discriminatory arrangements later found to be in breach of EC law can claim retrospectively. The time limit runs from the date when the Member State fully implements the EC directive (*Emmott* v. *Minister for Social Welfare and anor*). As regards discriminatory maximum ages for entitlement to RP, this was 16 January 1990. A claim one month and twelve days after this date was not out of time. The redundancy had occurred in August 1985 (*Cannon* v. *Barnsley Metropolitan Borough Council*; see also *Rankin* v. *British Coal Corporation*). Prior to this it had been held by the EAT that there was no time limit on cases pursued under article 119 of the Treaty of Rome (*Stevens and ors* v. *Bexley Health Authority*; followed by an industrial tribunal in *Hughes* v. *Strathclyde Regional Council*). An industrial tribunal has jurisdiction to hear a case brought directly under EC law where the applicant has no remedy under domestic legislation, for example, exclusion from the right to a contractual RP because of being a part-time employee (*Secretary of State for Scotland and Greater Glasgow Health Board* v. *Wright and Hannah*). Similarly, a direct application under article 119 was possible for a woman over 60 who was not entitled to claim under British Law (*McKechnie* v. *UBM Building Supplies (Southern) Ltd*).

Where a claim is made in respect of unfair dismissal for redundancy, but there is no claim for a RP, the tribunal must give the parties the opportunity to call evidence and make representations if it is contemplating the award of a RP (*Ransomes Sims and Jeffries Ltd* v. *Tatterton*).

Where there is no dispute about entitlement and amount the matter is settled, providing the payment is calculated in accordance with the statutory rules. An employee may claim a payment, or any unpaid part of it, direct from the NI Fund after taking all reasonable steps (other than legal proceedings) to recover the payment from the employer, or when the employer is insolvent.[43] The Secretary of State then tries to pursue a claim against the employer. An employee refused a direct payment by the Secretary of State can contest the decision by applying to an industrial tribunal. There is also provision for the Secretary of State to challenge liability, or the amount of RP, by referring a claim to the tribunal.

## Rebates to employers

Prior to the commencement of s. 17 of the Employment Act 1989 in January 1990 there had been a system of rebates paid to employers making statutory redundancy payments. Originally these rebates

were paid to all such employers but the proportion of the RP re-
funded was reduced over the years, and then more latterly restricted
to small firms. The system of rebates has now been abolished
completely.

## Early and late leaving and notice

There can be mutual agreement to bring forward the termination
date. A second possibility is that the employee, under notice of
redundancy, and during the 'obligatory' notice period, gives notice
in writing to the employer to leave early. This notice does not have
to be of the length needed for termination – simply *some* notice
(*Ready Case Ltd* v. *Jackson*). The termination will still be held to be
a dismissal for redundancy. The 'obligatory' notice period is that
required by statute or contract, whichever is the longer. Where
the employer gives notice in excess of the obligatory amount, the
obligatory period is the later rather than the earlier part of the notice.
Some examples are given in table 6. Notice from the employee earlier
than the obligatory period will be treated as a resignation and will
result in a loss of entitlement to RP.

**Table 6**   Obligatory notice period – examples

| | Employee with five years' continuous employment | | | |
| *Example* | *Minimum statutory notice (weeks)* | *Contractual notice (weeks)* | *Actual notice (weeks)* | *Obligatory notice period (weeks)* |
| --- | --- | --- | --- | --- |
| 1 | 5 | 5 | 5 | 5 |
| 2 | 5 | 4 | 5 | 5 |
| 3 | 5 | 8 | 8 | 8 |
| 4 | 5 | 8 | 13 | Weeks 6–13 of the 13 week period |

An employer can give a further notice, which must be in writing and
be served before the employee's counter-notice expires, to tell the
employee to withdraw his counter-notice and work until the full
notice period expires. This notice must also state that unless the
employee complies, the employer will contest liability to pay RP.

Where such a case is pursued to an industrial tribunal, the tribunal will determine how much of the RP, if any, is payable.[44]

There can be mutual agreement to defer notice of termination. In *Mowlem (Northern) Ltd* v. *Watson*, the notice was suspended by mutual agreement and although there was no new leaving date, the right to a statutory RP was preserved. This was because the original notice of dismissal stood. Where there has been a strike during the notice period, an employer can require that the notice period be extended.[45]

The two-year period of qualifying employment must be measured to the 'relevant date' (see above, p. 136). A failure to give the statutory minimum notice required causes the relevant date to be postponed until the date on which the proper amount of notice would have expired, but this is true only for the purposes of determining the two-year qualifying period and length of employment for the RP calculation. The relevant date may be postponed even where an employee has accepted pay in lieu of notice because neither the acceptance of pay in lieu nor the waiving of notice rights can prevent the operation of the statutory provisions as regards the qualifying period for the right to a RP (*Staffordshire County Council* v. *Secretary of State for Employment*).

## Statutory exemption orders

Where an employer and one or more trades unions have a redundancy agreement, they may jointly apply to the Secretary of State for Employment to exempt certain employees from the statutory provisions. However, issues in dispute will still have to be dealt with by industrial tribunals.[46]

## Exclusion or reduction of RP on account of pension rights

Entitlement to a statutory RP may be excluded because of pension rights. Section 98 of EP(C)A allows the Secretary of State to make regulations for excluding the right to a statutory RP, or reducing the entitlement, where an employee is entitled to an occupational pension at the time of redundancy. The regulations, issued in 1965, specify that an employer may reduce or exclude a RP, should he so choose, where a pension is payable within 90 weeks of the termination of employment.[47] The pension scheme must be satisfactory as far as the Secretary of State for Employment is concerned and the pension must be payable for life (or commutable into a lump sum). The RP can be excluded altogether where the employee is entitled to a pension which is equal to at least a third of his annual pay and where he has a right to payment of the pension immediately upon termination of employment. Annual pay is determined by multiplying weekly pay by 52. Weekly pay is subject to the statutory limit, currently £205. Where the pension is less than a third of the employee's annual pay, the RP may be reduced by the formula:

$$\frac{\text{Annual pension}}{\frac{1}{3} \text{ annual pay}} \times 100$$

Thus, if annual pay is £9,000 and the annual pension is £2,000, the RP may be reduced by 67 per cent. Where pension is not payable immediately, but is payable in no more than 90 weeks' time, the same calculation is done but the weekly pension is multiplied by the appropriate number of weeks and the result added on. Where a RP is to be reduced or excluded, an employer must give the employee notice in writing of the intention to reduce or exclude, explain how it is to be done and state the amount which will be payable. The notice must be served within a reasonable time of the employer coming to know of the employee's claim for RP (*Stowe-Woodward BTR Ltd* v. *Beynon*). Three months was not reasonable.

In *British Telecommunications plc* v. *Burwell* the EAT decided that the regulations applied to a situation where a person was, at termination of employment, already in receipt of a pension (arising out of a previous termination). However, the Court of Appeal has held that this is not so (*Royal Ordnance plc* v. *Pilkington*).

## Extra-Statutory Payments

### Additions to the lump-sum RP

An employer must not make a payment which is less than the statutory amount but is at liberty to make a payment which is greater. Part of such a payment would be to meet statutory obligations and the remainder would be a voluntary payment (unless contractually required). Where extra-statutory payments are made, a refusal to give a recognized trades union information showing how the amounts are calculated may allow the union to make a successful claim under the bargaining information provisions of the

TULR(C)A[48] (*Transport and General Workers' Union* v. *BP Chemicals Ltd*). The TURERA provides that the method of calculating extra-statutory RPs is added to the list of information which has to be given to representatives of a recognized trades union (see above, p. 115). There are four ways in which an employer can make additions to the statutory RP.

*Including those who would otherwise receive no payment*   Any full-time employee who does not have two years of continuous employment with his present employer is not entitled to a statutory RP, but an employer who wishes to do so is free to make a payment to such an employee. Full-time in this context means 16 or more hours per week. Any employee who works under a contract for eight or more hours per week, but less than 16, will not be entitled to a statutory RP until five years have passed. Again, such people can be included, as can those working less than eight hours per week, who would never qualify for a statutory payment because they do not have any continuous employment (in the legal sense of the term). Similarly, those excluded by virtue of having reached the age of 65 years (or such lower, non-discriminatory NRA as might exist) may be included.

*Including employment which does not count under the statutory scheme*   It was noted earlier that only 20 years of employment may be counted for calculation purposes. An employer wishing to make a redundancy package more attractive than that required by law, therefore, may choose to count all the employee's service. In the case of long serving employees this could result in a substantial addition to the statutory payment. It was also noted that employment before the employee's eighteenth birthday did not count. Again, this could be counted, and might be particularly beneficial in the case of younger employees being made redundant.

*Adopting a wider definition of pay for calculation purposes*   Employers may adopt a wider, and therefore more generous, definition of pay than that used in the statutory scheme. For example, and perhaps most obviously, an employer can dispense with the statutory limit on the amount of weekly pay which is to be used in the calculation. The limit is currently £205. Also, an employer can include overtime and perhaps other, typically non-contractual components of pay, in order to provide a payment based on average weekly earnings.

Furthermore, an employer can take account of non-monetary benefits received by the employee, such as provision of a company car, free meals or free accommodation. As noted earlier, these are likely to be excluded from the statutory definition of a week's pay. Moreover, an employer may enhance the redundancy package by allowing redundant employees to retain certain benefits (for example, cheap insurance or mortgages, discount off the prices of company products and so on) for a limited period after the redundancy.

*Altering the computation formula* Employers sometimes alter the computation formula by applying a percentage increase to the statutory payment. Alternatively, a fixed sum can be added. It is also quite common for there to be an additional sum paid for each year of employment. Finally, an employer may substitute a different scale altogether, such as that in table 7, which leaves out of account the age of the employee. The effect of the substitute scale is shown for an employee aged 62 years with 1, 10 and 20 years' service respectively.

**Table 7**  Substituting a different scale for the computation of redundancy payments – an example

| Years of service | Statutory scheme – number of weeks' pay per year for a person aged 62 years | Substitute scheme – number of weeks' pay per year |
|---|---|---|
| 1–9 | $1\frac{1}{2}$ | 2 |
| 10–19 | $1\frac{1}{2}$ | 3 |
| 20 or more | $1\frac{1}{2}$ | 4 |

| Employee aged 62 years – years' service | Statutory RP[a] (£) | Substitute RP[a] (£) |
|---|---|---|
| 1 | 300 | 400 |
| 10 | 3,000 | 6,000 |
| 20 | 6,000 | 16,000 |

[a] The employee's pay is assumed to be £200 per week.

An employer wishing to make the redundancy package as attractive as possible may feel that reducing the RP because of the payment of pension (subject to the pensions and RP rules outlined above, see pp. 145–6) is likely to be counter-productive.

## Other forms of payment

Four other types of payment are quite common, although the fourth type applies where redundancy has been avoided.

*Unemployment pay* Such payments by an employer who has made an employee redundant are not widespread. They are paid if the redundant person remains unemployed, and are usually paid as a weekly amount. The formula adopted often fixes the amount of unemployment pay so that the individual has two-thirds of former average earnings or less frequently, 80 per cent. However, state unemployment benefit is counted, so that company unemployment pay makes up the difference between state benefits and the specified level of earnings.

*Retention bonuses* These are paid in the context of a plant closure where an employee is asked to remain in post after most of the redundancies have occurred in order to assist in the safe and efficient rundown of the plant.

*Pension improvements* To encourage older workers to accept redundancy, entitlement to pension benefits is often enhanced. The pension scheme must first of all allow early payment of benefits on grounds of redundancy. This is often done at age 50 or 55. Unlike the state scheme, however, the pensionable age must not be discriminatory on grounds of sex, and this applies to early payment as well as to NRA (*Barber* v. *Guardian Royal Exchange Assurance Group*). Next there is the question of enhancement. This is done by crediting the employee with more years of pensionable service than they have actually accrued. Where the employee is within a few years of achieving the service which would result in a full pension, the missing amount of years may be credited in full. Thus, for example, someone aged 60 with 35 years' pensionable service (in a scheme where 40 years is the maximum), might be able to retire immediately on a full pension. Where an employee is within a year of the age of which an early, enhanced pension becomes payable, some redundancy schemes will allow a postponement of the redundancy until the employee's next birthday. Usually, such provisions are accompanied by a requirement to accept whatever work the employer may be able to offer in the intervening period.

*Redeployment payments* Where a person is transferred within the company to a lower-paid job, a common response is to protect his or her pay for some specified period. This is known as red circling. Normal pay increases can be withheld over a period of time so that eventually the personal pay rate is absorbed into the standard pay for the position, without the individual having suffered a reduction in money wages. To provide a defence against equal pay claims, it should be made clear what part of pay is protected and why, and for what length of time. This situation can be distinguished from that in *McCree* v. *London Borough of Tower Hamlets* (absorption of a pay supplement) and it is perhaps unlikely that it would be caught by the Wages Act. However, obtaining the employee's prior agreement in writing might be a prudent step.

If the transfer is between sites, it may be necessary to make payments to ease the difficulty of moving. Most of these payments would be to reimburse the employee for costs associated with the move, for example, travel expenses, removal costs, house sale and purchase costs and rent for temporary accommodation. In addition, some payment is often made to compensate for the upheaval caused to the employee and his or her family. Appropriately, this is known as a disturbance payment.

In a number of industries, such as shipbuilding and coal, there have been statutory redundancy schemes which have replaced or added to the basic statutory scheme.[49] An example is given here to illustrate one of the best packages available. It is taken from British Steel in the 1980s. The current RP earnings limit of £205 per week is assumed for comparison purposes. No limit was applied in the British Steel Scheme, 50 per cent was added to the statutory amount and there was an entitlement to a maximum of 23 weeks' severance pay (see table 8).

In addition, the Iron and Steel Employees' Re-adaptation Benefits Scheme,[50] operated by the European Community, provided the following benefits:

- make-up of earnings on redeployment or on acceptance of a lower-paid job outside British Steel;
- unemployment benefit for those remaining unemployed, or if the employee was aged 55 or over, make-up of earnings;

**Table 8** Example of a generous redundancy payments scheme – British Steel

| | | British Steel[a] | | | |
|---|---|---|---|---|---|
| Earnings per week | Statutory RP | RP | 50% Supplement[b] | EGP[c] | Total |
| 200 | 6,000 | 6,000 | 3,000 | 4,600 | 13,600 |
| 300 | 6,150 | 9,000 | 4,500 | 6,900 | 20,400 |
| 400 | 6,150 | 12,000 | 6,000 | 9,200 | 27,200 |

[a] Assumption: the worker is in a manual grade job, is 62 years old and has 20 years' service (that is, 30 weeks' pay for RP purposes). He is entitled to 23 weeks' *ex gratia* payment (EGP – see note [c]).
[b] This is an extra-statutory addition equal to 50 per cent of the statutory amount.
[c] This is an additional severance payment of 23 weeks' pay, known as an *ex gratia* payment (EGP).

- training benefit for those going on approved training courses; and
- resettlement and other grants for those redeployed elsewhere in British Steel.

Finally, an early, enhanced pension was available at 55, with the option of commuting any EC make-up payments into a lump sum in order to buy additional pensionable service.

Certain highly-profitable firms in the private sector have been able to offer good packages without external finance. Examples include ICI and British Telecom. The latter was reported (in May 1992) as offering a RP of £70,000 to middle managers with 20 years' service earning £25,000 per year. Some payments were reported to be as high as £100,000, excluding the pension, with typical payments being between £30,000 and £40,000. In addition, the package contained training vouchers worth £1,000 and three months' guaranteed work through an employment agency. Twenty-five per cent of salary was payable as a bonus if an employee left before 31 July 1992. At the time, the statutory RP scheme provided for a maximum of £6,150.

## Guarantee Pay

The EP(C)A requires that there shall be a daily guarantee payment where the employer is unable to provide any work at all during a day when the employee would normally be required to work.[51] Crown employment is included but the armed forces and police service are excluded, as are share fishermen and employees ordinarily working outside Great Britain. One month's qualifying employment is needed and any employee on a fixed-term contract of three months or less, or on a specific task contract expected to last for three months or less, is excluded, unless there is already more than three months' continuous employment.

If the failure to provide work stems from industrial action in the employer's firm or any associated employer's firm, no payment will be due. Nor will it be due if suitable alternative employment (even if not permitted by the contract) is unreasonably refused, or if the employee does not conform to the employer's requirements relating to availability for work. The amount of daily payment is the number of normal hours multiplied by the hourly rate, subject to a statutory maximum, currently £14.10 but reviewed annually. No payment is due where there are 'no normal working hours on the day in question'.[52] The maximum number of days' guarantee pay is five in any three-month period. An employee may complain to an industrial tribunal that his employer has not paid part or all of the guarantee payment. This complaint must be made within three months of the day to which the application relates. Any remuneration for the day may be offset against the liability to pay statutory guarantee pay and vice versa. Where there is a collective agreement on guarantee pay, and at the request of the parties, the Minister may issue an Order exempting from the statutory provisions the employees covered by that agreement, but the agreement must provide for disputes to be resolved by independent arbitration or by industrial tribunals.[53] Guarantee pay has no bearing on the issue of whether the employer has a right under the contract to dispense with some or all of the employee's pay during a lay-off or short-time working when there is insufficient work. This will depend on the terms of the contract.

# Insolvency[54]

## *Rights of employees*

Insolvency rights fall into two categories:

- Some debts are given priority (up to a statutory maximum which may be changed from time to time by the Secretary of State).

• Some debts can be paid out of the NI Fund.

*Priority debts*  These include:

a  statutory guarantee payments;
b  remuneration payable on suspension on medical grounds;
c  payment for time off for union duties or to look for work or arrange training on being made redundant;
d  remuneration payable under a protective award;
e  payment for time off for ante-natal care;
f  statutory sick pay;
g  up to four months' wages or salary;
h  accrued holiday pay;
i  contractual sick pay and holiday pay.

*Debts which may be claimed from the NI Fund*  These are:

a  Arrears of pay for up to and including eight weeks. Pay includes wages, salaries, bonuses, commission, overtime pay and the statutory items (a)–(e) in the priority debts above. The maximum earnings limit, currently £205 per week, applies.
b  Holiday pay for up to and including six weeks – again the maximum earnings limit applies. The entitlement must have occurred within the previous 12 months.
c  Pay for the statutory notice period or compensation for the employer's failure to give proper statutory notice (again the earnings limit applies).
d  Unpaid basic award of unfair dismissal compensation
e  Reasonable reimbursement of apprentices' or articled clerks' fees
f  Statutory maternity pay, statutory sick pay and statutory redundancy pay. (These may also be met from the NI Fund in certain cases where there is no insolvency).[55]

*Claims*  Claims in the first instance should go to the employer's representative on prescribed forms. Debts in addition to those above will be considered by that representative, but will not be paid from public funds. The legislation however does safeguard pension contributions left unpaid by an insolvent employer. The pension scheme administrator applies to the employer's representative in the first instance, but ultimately the NI Fund may pay. As regards any of the debts claimed from the NI Fund, a complaint may be made to a tribunal that the Secretary of State has failed to make a payment, or that the payment is less than the amount it should be. The EP(C)A provided that the Secretary of State must await a statement from the receiver or liquidator of the amount payable before making such a payment, unless there was likely to be unreasonable delay. Section 18 of the Employment Act 1989 allows the Secretary of State to make payments without a statement if he feels that a statement is not necessary. Moreover, s. 19 makes it clear that where payments are made to employees out of the NI Fund the right to a priority claim on the assets of the employer is transferred to the Secretary of State. In the case of unpaid pension contributions an application will be made by an officer of the pension scheme, while in respect of other debts by the ex-employee the time limit for claims is three months from the Secretary of State's decision. There is no hours qualification for the insolvency rights, nor any qualifying period of employment.

## Insolvency and business transfers[56]

The fact that a company is insolvent, in receivership or about to cease trading does not preclude the operation of legislation relating to business transfers (*Teesside Times Ltd* v. *Drury*). Where an insolvency practitioner manages the company and succeeds in selling all or part of it as a going concern there is likely to be the transfer of an undertaking. By contrast, the legislation may not apply where a business is broken up and the assets sold, since there would be no transfer of a going concern.

A receiver who is also a manager is called an administrative receiver.[57] Where appointed voluntarily he is an agent of the company and has authority to continue its business and to sell it. His appointment is not a transfer under the Transfer Regulations, nor does it terminate the contracts of employment of employees. The above also is true of an administrator under the Insolvency Act 1986 (appointed under a court administration order as an expert to manage the affairs, business and property of the company) and of a liquidator appointed following a voluntary liquidation.

The position in relation to compulsory liquidation is different. The liquidator is appointed by the court and is an agent of the court. His appointment automatically terminates contracts of employment. If he wishes to continue the employment of employees he must employ them. Moreover, the acquired rights directive apparently does not apply to insolvency proceedings supervised by a judicial authority (*Abels* v. *The Administrative Board of the Bedrijfsvereniging voor de Metaal Industrie en de Electrotechnische Industrie*; *D'Urso and ors* v. *Ercole Marelli Elletromeccanica Generale SpA and ors*). In the UK, this would mean a compulsory liquidation (or in the case of an individual, personal bankruptcy) but the position is uncertain and generally it is assumed that the Transfer Regulations would apply.[58] In practice, there is often no actual business to transfer, merely a collection of assets.

Finally, there is the question of the hiving down of a business by a receiver, administrator or liquidator, that is, the separation of the employees from the business in order to make the latter more attractive to potential buyers. This involves:

- creating a wholly-owned subsidiary;
- transferring the business to it;
- retaining the employees in the original company but lending them to the subsidiary;
- disposing of the subsidiary business by transfer or by sale of shares; and
- dismissing the employees from the original company before disposal of the subsidiary.

Although no provision for this is made in the acquired rights directive, the Transfer Regulations have the effect of postponing the transfer on hiving down until either disposal of the share capital of the subsidiary to a buyer or disposal of the subsidiary business to a buyer.[59] The initial transfer to the subsidiary therefore is not covered by the regulations so that contracts of employment do not transfer. However, one view has it that the rule in *Litster* (see above, p. 86) applies even in the context of a dismissal following a postponed transfer after hiving down – so causing a transfer of liability to the transferee if there is no ETO reason – but this remains untested.[60]

## Redundancy Payments, Taxation and Social Security

### Termination payments and taxation

Contractual termination payments normally will be taxable as income under Schedule E, but non-contractual payments are treated separately, attracting a measure of tax relief.[61] Under the current provisions the first £30,000 is tax-free.[62] Statutory and genuine extra-statutory RPs fall to be treated in the same way.[63] Where something less than contractual notice is given, and there is no contractual right to make a payment in lieu of notice, any payment is likely to attract tax relief. However, it will be included as a compensation payment to be aggregated with the RP for purposes of the £30,000 limit on compensation which is subject to tax relief. To the extent that wages in lieu of notice are technically damages for breach of contract they should be paid net, although in practice are usually paid gross. Since wages in lieu will vary from individual to individual according to notice requirements, a standard wages in lieu payment (for example, 12 weeks' pay) may be regarded as a RP, thus leaving unfulfilled the duty to pay wages in lieu (see p. 125).

*Ex gratia* payments which are compensation for loss of office or employment should also be subject to tax relief, but again they will need to be aggregated along with the RP and any other termination payments not charged under Schedule E in applying the £30,000 ceiling to the amount of tax-free compensation. The early payment of retirement benefits should not affect the tax treatment of compensation for loss of office or employment.[64]

In contrast to compensation for loss of employment, *ex gratia* payments on retirement or death will be subject to the tax rules governing pension schemes, since they are 'a relevant benefit' under s. 612 of the Income and Corporation Taxes Act 1988 (ICTA). Thus, a lump sum retirement benefit will be taxable unless it qualifies for exemption under the rules: these allow tax-free payments of up to 150 per cent of final salary.

### Termination payments and Unemployment Benefit

Whatever the size of the RP an employee's right to claim NI Unemployment Benefit is not affected and this applies to both statutory and extra-statutory redundancy payments. It should be noted, however, that other payments (for example, *ex gratia* payments) may affect such entitlement and might best be replaced by an increased RP. Pay in lieu of notice or pay during a notice period will remove the entitlement to Unemployment Benefit for the period of the notice (or what should have been the period of the notice). However, what if the employee waives his notice rights – in which case there is neither notice nor wages in lieu – in exchange for a more generous RP?[65] In theory, entitlement to Unemployment Benefit should remain intact. Protective awards under the TULR(C)A, however, will remove entitlement to Unemployment Benefit, although they will not be subject to tax and NI.[66]

A person aged 55 years or more who is made redundant and is in receipt of an occupational pension will have his or her Unemployment Benefit reduced by the amount of pension in excess of

£35 per week.[67] The pension figure to be used for the calculation is the gross amount.[68]

Someone who volunteers for redundancy will not lose any of their entitlement to Unemployment Benefit on the grounds that they left their employment voluntarily. The Social Security Contributions and Benefits Act 1992 specifically protects their entitlement.[69] In the absence of such protection it seems that some entitlement to Unemployment Benefit would be lost (*Crewe* v. *Social Security Commissioner*).

Where the employee is temporarily laid off or put on short-time rather than dismissed by reason of redundancy, the contract of employment is likely to be regarded as suspended rather than terminated and there generally will be an entitlement to Unemployment Benefit. Where certain conditions are met, lay-off or short-time working can provide entitlement to a statutory RP, in which case termination is a prerequisite and Unemployment Benefit will be payable on the same basis as in a redundancy (see pp. 131–3). If the employee who is laid off or put on short-time does not (or is not entitled to) claim a statutory RP, he or she will be entitled to Unemployment Benefit, subject to being available for work. Thus, Unemployment Benefit will be denied where the employer is making a guarantee payment (such as under a collective agreement) because such a payment will require the employee to be available for work with that employer. The employee cannot be *generally* available for work as the Unemployment Benefit rules require.

Bearing this in mind, it might be better for guaranteed week agreements to guarantee pay equal to a proportion of a week's pay (say four days out of five) and to require employees to be available for work for those four (specified) days only. This would leave the employee free to claim Unemployment Benefit on the fifth day when he would be generally available for work. This can be contrasted with the normal guaranteed week agreement which provides for a proportion of pay (say, four fifths) but requires the employee to be available for work for the whole week, so denying entitlement to Unemployment Benefit. It can be seen that as long as the employer does not need the employee to be available for the whole week the former arrangement benefits the employee without cost to the employer.[70] Many guaranteed week agreements have provision for the suspension of the agreement in specified circumstances. Where the agreement is suspended, the employee should be entitled to Unemployment Benefit. An employee will not be entitled to

Unemployment Benefit for any day in which he is in receipt of a statutory guarantee payment (see pp. 151–2).

Unemployment Benefit will not be payable where a redundancy is also an unfair dismissal (see above, chapter 7) and compensation has been awarded in respect of a period of unemployment. Where Unemployment Benefit has already been paid, the Department of Employment will recoup the benefit.[71] This will be done by the industrial tribunal prescribing a period in respect of which the employer must not pay compensation to the employee until the Department has reclaimed what it is due. Once recoupment is effected, the employer pays the balance to the employee. The payment of compensation other than that relating to the prescribed period need not be delayed by the recoupment process – this amount may be paid immediately after the tribunal's decision is promulgated.

### Termination payments and Income Support

Unemployment Benefit is payable on the basis of contribution record and eligibility in terms of the scheme's rules, but does not take into account level of income. By contrast, Income Support is a means-tested benefit which replaced Supplementary Benefit in 1988.[72] Entitlement is based on a comparison between the claimant's income on the one hand and an individually-assessed but statutorily-derived minimum level on the other, the shortfall being the amount of Income Support which is due. Allowances are awarded for individuals, couples and children and premiums are added for certain circumstances, for example, disability, age and so on. A person who has been made redundant may be able to obtain Income Support if they are not entitled to Unemployment Benefit,[73] and as with Unemployment Benefit, the penalties attached to voluntary leaving will not be brought into play just because the employee volunteered for redundancy. The penalty in relation to Income Support is a 40 per cent reduction in the personal allowances; 20 per cent in certain circumstances.[74]

However, redundancy may affect a claimant's entitlement in two important ways. First, there are rules about the amount of capital the claimant and his partner may have.[75] Where this amount exceeds £8,000, no Income Support will be payable, and between £3,000 and £8,000 the capital results in notional income being included in the Income Support calculation. Thus, capital of £4,000 is assumed to bring in income of £4 per week and £5,000 is assumed to bring in £8 per week. Disposal of a RP can result in the RP still being included in the Income Support calculation as 'notional capital'.[76] Second, where the redundant employee is entitled to an occupational or personal pension, that amount will be counted in full in the Income Support calculation.[77]

## Notes

1 EP(C)A, s. 81(4). Continuous employment is defined in chapter 7 (pp. 92–3). Overseas employment will count for RP qualifying period and calculation purposes if the employee remains an employed earner as defined in the NI scheme.
2 Employment Act 1989.
3 EP(C)A, s. 151(4).
4 Part-time employees are excluded by virtue of the rules for determining continuous employment. These are laid down in EP(C)A, schedule 13.
5 EP(C)A, s. 144(2).
6 Crown servants are excluded by the absence of express inclusion (unlike in respect of unfair dismissal legislation – EP(C)A, s. 138(1)).
7 EP(C)A, s. 141(4). The employee's base is to be ascertained by looking at the terms of the contract and over the whole period contemplated by the contract (*Wilson* v. *Maynard Shipping Consultants AB*).
8 EP(C)A, s. 141(3).
9 EP(C)A, ss. 99(2) and 114.
10 EP(C)A, s. 100(2).
11 Dock Work Act 1989; Dock Work (Compensation Payments Scheme) Regulations, SI 1989/1111, under s. 5(1) of the 1989 Act.
12 National Health Service and Community Care Act 1990, s. 66(2) and schedule 10. Merchant seamen were excluded by the Secretary of State by an order under EP(C)A, s. 149(1) but are now included by virtue of SI 1990/1583, which revoked the Redundancy Payments (Exclusion of Merchant Seamen) Order, SI 1968/1201.
13 Under EP(C)A, s. 115, for example, Redundancy Payments Office Holders Regulations, SI 1965/2007 including, for example, registrars of births and deaths; and the Redundancy Payments Termination of Employment Regulations, SI 1965/2022, including, for example, chief constables.
14 Employment Protection (Offshore Employment) Order, SI 1976/766 as amended by SI 1977/588 and SI 1981/208. This extends RP and unfair dismissal rights to employees on oil or natural gas rigs within British territorial waters or in designated areas of the continental shelf, with the exception of areas adjacent to Northern Ireland. The Employment (Continental Shelf) Act 1978 makes provision for those employed

further afield to be covered by British employment legislation if they are employed by British-based firms.

15   EP(C)A, s. 142(4).

16   In respect of RPs: EP(C)A, ss. 83 and 86; in respect of unfair dismissal: EP(C)A, ss. 55–56; and in respect of redundancy consultation: TULR(C)A, s. 298.

17   EP(C)A, s. 93(1).

18   EP(C)A, ss. 93(2)(3) and (4).

19   EP(C)A, ss. 82(2) and 92.

20   EP(C)A, s. 87.

21   Set out in EP(C)A, ss. 88–9.

22   EP(C)A, s. 82(5)(b).

23   286 IDS Brief 3–5.

24   281 IDS Brief 8.

25   EP(C)A, s. 84(1).

26   EP(C)A, schedule 13, para. 17.

27   Transfer of Undertakings (Protection of Employment) Regulations, SI 1981/1794.

28   EP(C)A, schedule 13, para. 12.

29   EP(C)A, schedule 13, para. 7.

30   Strike is defined, for the purpose of EP(C)A, schedule 13, in para. 24(1) of schedule 13.

31   Redundancy Payments (Local Government) (Modification) Order, SI 1983/1160, as amended by SI 1985/1872, 1988/907, 1989/532, 1990/826 and 1991/818 under s. 149 of EP(C)A. A number of bodies, apart from local authorities, are to be treated as local authorities, and like local authorities, all are deemed to be associated employers for RP purposes. Organizations not specified can be similarly regarded but only if they perform current local authority functions as contractors or agents (*West Midlands Residuary Body* v. *Deebank*).

32   EP(C)A, schedule 4, para. 2. It is a payment for loss of security. It is not intended to be unemployment pay (*Lloyd* v. *Brassey*).

33   EP(C)A, schedule 14, para. 8(1)(c).

34   EP(C)A, s. 148. The 1993 review did not lead to an increase.

35   The Employment Act 1989, s. 16 amended EP(C)A, schedule 4, para. 4(2).

36   Local authorities may make enhanced RPs under s. 111 of the Local Government Act 1972 but the enhancement is limited by regulations made under the Superannuation Act 1972.

37   EP(C)A, schedule 14, para. 7(1)(k)(l) and 7(2).

38   See EP(C)A, schedule 14, para. 2(a) and (b). For overtime to be contractual, the employer must be obliged to provide it *and* the employee be required to work it.

39   See Grunfeld, C., *The Law of Redundancy*, 3rd edition, London: Sweet & Maxwell, 1989, p. 268 ff. for a fuller discussion.

40  EP(C)A, s. 102.

41  EP(C)A, s. 120.

42  These are claims under EP(C)A, s. 112. The more general limit of six years is laid down in s. 5 of the Limitation Act 1980.

43  The Redundancy Fund was merged with the National Insurance Fund by the Employment Act 1990. Insolvency for this purpose is defined in EP(C)A, s. 106(5).

44  EP(C)A, s. 85.

45  EP(C)A, s. 110.

46  EP(C)A, s. 96. See *Southern Electricity Board* v. *Collins* at p. 88, above, and Redundancy Payments (Exemption) (No. 1) Order, SI 1970/354 and Redundancy Payments (Centrax Group) (Exemption) Order, SI 1969/207.

47  Redundancy Payments (Pensions) Regulations, SI 1965/1932.

48  TULR(C)A, s. 183. The claim is made to the Central Arbitration Committee.

49  The Redundant Mineworkers' Payment Scheme, which expired in 1987, had been established under the Coal Industry Acts 1965–85. For those aged under 55 it provided £1,000 per year of service in addition to any statutory RP. The Shipbuilding Redundancy Payments Scheme also expired in 1987. It provided lump sums, make-up payments, unemployment benefits and training grants.

50  European Committees (Iron and Steel Employees' Re-adaptation Benefits Scheme) Regulations, SI 1974/908 and SI 1979/954, as amended.

51  EP(C)A, s. 12.

52  EP(C)A, s. 14(1).

53  EP(C)A, s. 18.

54  Insolvency Act 1986.

55  On statutory maternity pay see: Social Security Contributions and Benefits Act 1992 (SSCBA), ss. 164–71 and schedule 13 and the Statutory Maternity Pay (General) Regulations, SI 1986/1960 as amended. On statutory sick pay see the SSCBA ss. 151–63 and schedules 11–12 and the Statutory Sick Pay (General) Regulations SI 1982/894 as amended. See also the Social Security Administration Act 1992. On statutory redundancy pay see: EP(C)A, s. 106.

56  For a fuller discussion of this subject see McMullen, *Business Transfers and Employee Rights*, pp. 218–31.

57  Insolvency Act 1986, s. 29(2). Where voluntarily appointed, an administrative receiver will be personally liable for the contracts of employment of employees adopted by him or entered into by him, but will be entitled to an indemnity from out of the company's assets (Insolvency Act 1986, s. 44).

58  McMullen, *Business Transfers and Employee Rights*, p. 221.

59  Reg. 4.

60  McMullen, *Business Transfers and Employee Rights*, pp. 226–7.
61  They fall to be dealt with under s. 148 of the Income and Corporation Taxes Act (ICTA) 1988 instead of the normal charging provision in s. 19.
62  ICTA, s. 188(4) as amended by Finance Act 1988, s. 74.
63  Inland Revenue, *Ex Gratia Awards Made on Termination of an Office or Employment by Retirement or Death*, Statement of Practice SP 13/91, London: Inland Revenue, 1991. Statutory RPs are exempt from Schedule E charging by virtue of ICTA, s. 579. They are charged under s. 148 (with relief under s. 188) by virtue of s. 580.
64  Inland Revenue, *Ex Gratia Awards*.
65  This is permissible under EP(C)A, s. 49(3).
66  TULR(C)A, s. 189. See above, pp. 117–18 and *Reported Decisions of the National Insurance Commissioners*, R(U) 7/80.
67  The Social Security (No. 2) Act 1980, s. 5 provided for a reduction in Unemployment Benefit if a person was 60 or over if payments made by way of an occupational pension exceeded a prescribed sum for any week. The Social Security (Unemployment Benefit) (Abatement for Occupational Pension Payments) Regulations, SI 1981/73, set that sum at £35. The Social Security Act 1988, s. 7 substituted 55 for 60 in s. 5 of the 1980 Act. These provisions are now contained in s. 30 of the Social Security Contributions and Benefits Act 1992.
68  *Reported Decisions of the National Insurance Commissioners*, R(U) 8/83.
69  s. 28(4): 'a person who has been dismissed . . . by reason of redundancy . . . after volunteering or agreeing so to be dismissed shall not be deemed to have left his employment voluntarily'. The disqualification period was increased from 6 to 13 weeks by the Social Security Act 1986, s. 43, which also provided that those weeks of payment were to be forfeited rather than merely postponed as hitherto. Since 1988 the disqualification period has been six months.
70  This idea is put forward in Bourn, *Redundancy Law and Practice*, London: Butterworths, 1983, pp. 241–2.
71  Employment Protection (Recoupment of Unemployment Benefit and Supplementary Benefit) Regulations, SI 1977/674 as amended. For a worked example see Lewis, P., *Practical Employment Law: A Guide for Human Resource Managers*, Oxford: Blackwell, 1992, pp. 316–17.
72  Social Security Contributions and Benefits Act 1992; Income Support (General) Regulations, SI 1987/1967.
73  Indeed, they could obtain both Income Support and Unemployment Benefit if after receiving Unemployment Benefit their income was still below the minimum level.
74  Income Support (General) Regulations, reg. 22.
75  Regs. 45–53 and schedule 10.
76  Reg. 51.
77  Reg. 2(1).

# Conclusions

Change means that employers from time to time need to make adjustments to their demand for labour. Where demand is reduced, redundancy may be an outcome. Ultimately, the problem of how to manage redundancy is the problem of how to accommodate change. Experience in the UK and elsewhere shows that the starting point is often whether labour demand can be reduced *without* the need for redundancy. Typically this is achieved by reducing labour supply through measures such as cutting hours of work and the use of early retirement. Marketing-led approaches to the problem start from the premise that turnover and profits can be increased by amounts sufficient to sustain the demand for labour.

National schemes for the management of redundancy quite commonly lay down procedures for consultation with workers' representatives and for the provision of information to public authorities. Both of these developments have as their aims the avoidance or minimization of redundancy and mitigation of the effects. The latter aim usually is met through a combination of financial support for the redundant employee and assistance with attempts to find another job. What has developed is a three-pronged approach:[1]

- a requirement to submit plans for redundancy to workers' representatives and public authorities;
- attention to averting or minimizing redundancy, with varying types of public assistance where necessary; and
- measures to help mitigate the effects of redundancies.

It is probably in Western Europe and Japan that this approach is most developed.

The above policy elements are often present: what tends to vary between countries is the emphasis. Thus, there is a stronger focus on avoidance in Japan, but greater procedural requirements tend to exist in Western European countries. By contrast, in North America there is more reliance on unemployment insurance and adjustment through the free market mechanism. What also varies is the institutional picture; for example, the relative significance of legal controls on the one hand and regulation through collective agreements on the other.

The role of the state is a major difference when the international view is taken. It is relatively minor in North America but quite substantial in, for example, France. Also, the state role itself may differ in emphasis. Thus, whereas in France the public authorities' role involves examining the redundancy decision in an attempt to avoid or minimize redundancies, in Australia there is an important public role through tribunals and arbitration in setting redundancy terms. Third-party involvement of both the French and Australian types is likely to reduce the conflict over redundancy.

Another major aspect of the approach to the management of redundancy at national level is division of the costs of redundancy between the parties. Is the division fair as between employers, employees and the public interest? But there is more than equity at stake: the arrangements need to be compatible with the efficient functioning of the economy. Thus they need to:

- permit increased business efficiency by not discouraging redundancies which are necessary;
- encourage redundant workers to find new jobs; and
- be an effective use of public resources.

In terms of extremes, the management of redundancy may be said to involve the 'head in the sand' approach at one end of the spectrum and the 'frontier mentality' at the other. The former involves a refusal to admit the inevitability and necessity of redundancy in a dynamic environment, the latter is based on the idea that redundancy should take its natural course and that those displaced should head for the frontier and break new ground.

The effects of undue restrictions on redundancy are likely to result in low labour productivity because firms are prevented from fixing proper staffing levels and because there is inadequate mobility of labour. Moreover, such systems are likely to have excessive bureaucracies of public officials. The management of redundancy in Italy has been criticized for having both of the above features. There is also the difficulty in practice of deciding whether redundancies really are necessary, and if so, how many, as the Japanese courts have found. Any public perspective clearly would have to achieve some sort of balance between the competing interests of business performance and employee security.

Thus, there are major questions about a policy based on increased public control, implying minimization of the number of redundancies and extensive redeployment within the firm. It is not likely to ensure the more effective use of human and other resources and it may result in greater public bureaucracy. Also, it may be unenforceable. It assumes that public officials, most of whom are without business experience, have sufficient knowledge and understanding to be able to perform such a role. The biggest difficulty, however, is whether such an approach can work during periods of generalized structural change and/or prolonged recession. It is difficult to envisage how firms could retain surplus labour for long periods, or in situations where market competition is at its fiercest, without substantial employment subsidies from the public purse. The need for an injection of public money raises the question of whether it is better to subsidize labour surpluses or commit resources to national initiatives such as retraining, skills enhancement, geographical mobility measures and better state pensions.

These are the broad policy issues at the national level. It may be that no approach is capable of working in the context of prolonged recession, and it is difficult to assess which approaches seem to have been most successful. However, two tentative conclusions can be drawn for the UK in respect of policy at both national and enterprise levels. First, the UK places less emphasis on redundancy avoidance than do some countries. For employers and employees (and where applicable, trades unions) this raises the question of whether the array of other responses, and particularly reductions in hours (weekly, yearly or working life), might warrant closer scrutiny. Judicious use of the National Insurance system by the government could provide financial encouragement to employers. Second, the UK places more emphasis on lump sum RPs than do other countries. Could the package for those intending to stay in the labour market be more broadly-based to include retraining, enhancement of skills, job search assistance etc?

The best employers seek to avoid redundancies where possible and provide broad-based packages including generous RPs. Many firms, particularly small and medium-sized ones, will never be in a position to do all this, but taking the UK as a whole there is probably some scope for a movement in these directions.

## Note

1 *Workforce Reductions in Undertakings*, E. Yemin (Ed.), Geneva: International Labour Office, 1982. See pages 32–3.

# Appendix I

## Checklists for the Management of Redundancy

This appendix presents a number of checklists which are intended to assist managers in analysing and solving different types of redundancy problem. The figures in parentheses are page references showing where the issue is dealt with in the text. The areas covered by the checklists are:

- employer liability for statutory RPs;
- unfair dismissal for redundancy;
- consultation with trades unions; and
- redundancy strategy, policies and agreements.

### Checklist 1: Statutory Redundancy Payments

This checklist covers the main questions to be asked in order to determine whether an employer has liability for making a statutory redundancy payment to a worker, and the amount of any such payment which is due.

1 Is the worker an employee? (pp. 73–5)
2 Has the employee been dismissed? (pp. 129–30)
3 Is the reason for dismissal redundancy? (That is, does the employer require fewer employees?) (pp. 71–3)
4 Is the employee within the age limit? (p. 128)
5 Does the employee have sufficient continuous employment? (That is, does he have the necessary hours and years qualifications?) (pp. 128, 136–7)
6 Is the employee's occupation covered by the statutory RP scheme? (It may fall within one of the excluded occupational categories.) (pp. 128–9)
7 Has the claim for a RP been made in time? (pp. 142–3)
8 Does the employee ordinarily work in Great Britain? (p. 129)
9 Where the employee works under a fixed-term contract, has there been a waiver of RP rights? (p. 129)

10 Has the employee been offered alternative work which he has refused?
    If yes: (pp. 133–6)
    a  was the alternative work suitable?
    b  if so, was the employee reasonable to refuse it?

11 Has the employee been dismissed for industrial action or misconduct
    prior to the obligatory notice period? (p. 131)

12 Has misconduct by the employee taken place during (or been dis-
    covered during) the obligatory notice period? (p. 131)

13 Is the employee entitled to an occupational pension at the time of
    redundancy? (pp. 145–6)

14 Where an employee has been laid off or put on short-time working, has
    he followed the correct claims procedure? (pp. 131–3)

15 Where there has been a change of employer, has continuity of employ-
    ment been preserved by statute? (pp. 77–89)

16 Are there any weeks in which the employee has been employed which
    do not count towards the computation of his continuous employment?
    (pp. 128, 137)

17 Are any aspects of the employee's rewards to be excluded from the RP
    calculation e.g. earnings in excess of the statutory maximum weekly
    limit? (pp. 137, 140–2)

## Checklist 2:  Unfair Dismissal for Redundancy

This checklist covers the main questions an industrial tribunal will want
answered where a redundancy is alleged to be an unfair dismissal. In
defending a claim of unfair dismissal for redundancy an employer should
consider whether the industrial tribunal has jurisdiction and whether the
reason for the dismissal (i.e. redundancy) is being challenged, as well as the
fairness of selection and other aspects of the procedure.

### *Jurisdiction*

1 Can the applicant meet the eligibility criteria:
    a  two years' or more qualifying employment (which meets the hours
       rules)? (pp. 92–3)
    b  under NRA? (pp. 93–4)
    c  was the applicant an employee? (pp. 73–5)
    d  claim in time?   (three months) (p. 91)
    e  was the applicant dismissed? (p. 90)

### *Reason for dismissal*

2 Does the applicant accept redundancy as the reason? (pp. 71–3, 95–6)

## *Selection*

3 Who were the candidates for redundancy? (e.g. there were ten drivers two of whom had to be selected for redundancy) (p. 97)

4 What were the criteria for selection (e.g. length of employment, job experience, time-keeping and attendance record etc.) (pp. 100–1)

5 How were the criteria applied? (e.g. what weight was given to each criterion? Was length of service company, site or departmentally-based? Was alternative employment (and perhaps retraining) considered?) (pp. 99–100)

6 Who applied the criteria? Who made the selection decision? (This person probably will be a key witness.) (pp. 99–100)

7 Has there been a breach of an agreed procedure?

8 Has there been a breach of a customary arrangement?

⎫ If so, are there any special reasons justifying it? (pp. 97–8) ⎬

9 Has the selection been based on any of the following:
   a proposed or actual union membership or activity? (p. 97)
   b proposed or actual union non-membership? (p. 97)
   c race? (p. 102)
   d sex or pregnancy? (pp. 98, 102)

10 Is the dismissal unreasonable because of any other features of the selection process e.g. unreasonable selection criteria? (pp. 97–8)

## *Other aspects*

11 Is the dismissal unreasonable for any other reason(s);
   a was the employee consulted? (pp. 102–3)
   b where there is a recognized trades union, was the union consulted? (p. 103)
   c was there a bona fide search for suitable alternative work? (p. 103)

*Note*: Tribunals will want to be sure that the selection criteria adopted were fair and lawful, and that they were applied reasonably. Moreover, the tribunal will want to be satisfied that other aspects of the redundancy (e.g. consultation) were also reasonable.

## *Industrial tribunal procedure*

*Note*: See Handling an Industrial Tribunal case, chapter 12 in Lewis, P. *Practical Employment Law*: Blackwell, 1992.

12 Is the redundant employee making a claim for compensation in respect of a refusal to provide written reasons for dismissal? (pp. 109–10)

13 Where there is such a claim: (p. 109)
   a did the employee request written reasons;

    b   has the employer refused the request; and

    c   is the refusal unreasonable?

14   Has the employer provided written reasons within 14 days of the request? (p. 110)

15   Where selection is alleged to be on grounds of race or sex, has the questions procedure been used, and if so, has the employer replied? (A questions procedure exists under both the Sex Discrimination Act 1975 and the Race Relations Act 1976. It is intended to help complainants decide whether to institute proceedings, and to assist them in formulating and presenting their cases. There are prescribed forms which complainants may serve on defendants, and on which defendants may reply.)

16   Has the notice of appearance been entered within 14 days?

17   Should the case be proceeded with:

    a   has the strength of the case been assessed;

    b   what are the main arguments in the employer's case;

    c   is the evidence available to establish the necessary facts; and

    d   what is the likely cost of settlement compared with defending the case right through to the conclusion of a tribunal hearing?

18   Are there grounds for requesting a pre-hearing assessment?

19   Is the company prepared to settle, and if so, for how much?

20   Has ACAS been involved in any settlement and recorded it to prevent any further processing of the tribunal claim?

21   If the case is going ahead, should representation be in-house or external?

22   Is the representative familiar with:

    a   the relevant legislation;

    b   the circumstances of the case;

    c   industrial tribunal procedure; and

    d   the main principles established by case law?

23   Has the representative established the purpose of using each witness and document, and the sequence of evidence?

24   Are any witness orders needed?

25   Is the representative clear about the onus of proof at different points in the case?

26   Is it intended to make an application for costs, and if so, on what grounds?

27   Can a bundle of documents be agreed between the parties?

28   Have copies been provided for the tribunal, the applicant and the witness stand?

## Checklist 3:  Consultation with Trades Unions

1   Is the employer proposing to make one or more employees redundant? (pp. 113–14)

2 Is a trades union recognized in respect of any of these employees? (p. 113)
3 Is that trades union independent? (p. 112)
4 Has consultation begun as early as is required? (pp. 114–15)
5 Have the requirements for providing written information to union representatives been met? (p. 115)
6 Have the union's representations been considered? (p. 115)
7 Have the union's representations been replied to, with reasons where rejected? (p. 115)
8 Are there any special circumstances which make it not reasonably practicable to comply with some or all of the consultation requirements? (p. 116)
9 Where there are special circumstances, do the steps that have been taken to comply amount to all that is reasonably practicable? (p. 116)
10 Where there is a complaint by a union to an industrial tribunal, has it been lodged within the necessary period? (pp. 116–17)

## Checklist 4:  Redundancy Strategy, Policies and Agreements

This checklist covers strategy, policy issues and agreements with trades unions. The aim is to raise questions which managers will need to answer if their organization is to have an overall strategy for dealing with redundancy and a number of specific policies which flow from it.

### General strategy

1 Should policies be determined only when and if redundancy occurs or should they be determined in advance? (pp. 52–5)
2 Should policy-making be shared with a trades union and set out in an agreement? (pp. 55–9)
3 Does the organization have policies which cover:
 a the steps to be taken to minimize redundancies; (pp. 1–16)
 b consultation arrangements; (pp. 111–19)
 c selection criteria and methods; (pp. 96–102)
 d extra-statutory RPs (pp. 146–51); and
 e other measures, such as employee assistance? (pp. 120–5)

### Agreements with trades unions

4 What aspects of policy should be shared with a trades union? (p. 59)
5 Should agreements be reached in advance of redundancy, and if so, over what issues? (pp. 52–5)

6   Where there is an agreement, does it cover: (pp. 55–9)
   a   the intention and commitment of the parties;
   b   redundancy avoidance;
   c   consultation;
   d   selection;
   e   early retirement; and
   f   employee assistance?
7   Is there provision for:
   a   a right of appeal against selection; (pp. 59, 101)
   b   consideration of cases of hardship (p. 59); and
   c   interpretation, review and termination of the agreement? (p. 59)
8   Are any of the redundancy terms to be agreed with a trades union (including procedures) likely to become incorporated into individual employees' contracts of employment? (Where an agreement already exists – has this occurred?) (pp. 56–7)

## Voluntary redundancy

9   Should voluntary redundancy be used, and if so, how much extra finance will be needed? (pp. 17–38)
10  Are the circumstances likely to make the use of voluntary redundancy effective in practice? (pp. 25–8)
11  Where voluntary redundancy is to be used, have management built into their policy: (pp. 28–32)
   a   control over who is allowed to volunteer;
   b   control over selection from the pool of volunteers;
   c   control over the timing of individual departures;
   d   sufficient workforce data to ensure a match between post-redundancy operational needs and the composition of the retained workforce (e.g. in terms of numbers, skills and experience); and
   e   direct communication with the workforce (e.g. counselling)?
12  Where there is a trades union, can union agreement to support voluntary redundancy be obtained? (pp. 33–4)
13  Where there is a shortfall in the number of volunteers for redundancy, can management: (pp. 34–6)
   a   communicate the package more effectively to employees;
   b   exert more pressure upon potential volunteers;
   c   improve the financial package (e.g. through larger RPs and/or better enhancement of early pensions);
   d   reduce the perceived costs of volunteering (e.g. by providing greater assistance to employees in their labour market activities);
   e   use the pay system to show how the effects of volunteering will benefit the retained labour force and any trades union;
   f   put more pressure upon departmental management to prevent them dissuading people from volunteering;

g    include in the voluntary redundancy scheme some or all of those previously excluded, and/or allow the redundancy of volunteers previously refused it;

h    meet the shortfall through compulsory redundancy;

i    find other savings instead;

j    reduce the total savings needed (i.e. spread them over a longer period)?

## Other aspects of strategy

14    Where existing redundancy terms need to be altered, are any of them contractual? (pp. 56–7, 62–4)

15    Can the pay system be used to increase the acceptability of redundancy? (pp. 64, 65)

16    At what levels should different aspects of redundancy policy be implemented? (pp. 32, 62)

## Redundancy and business performance

17    Can different redundancy strategies be subjected to cost/benefit analysis in order to determine the best approach? (pp. 48–50)

18    Can redundancy be used as a means of improving productivity? (pp. 39–44)

19    What possibilities are there for using any of the following in order to achieve improved productivity and better financial performance: (pp. 39–44)

a    increased flexibility;

b    (wider) use of contractors;

c    reduced activity or services;

d    reorganization;

e    increased workload;

f    increased use of equipment.

20    Will redundancy and any changes accompanying it require: (pp. 44–8)

a    extra training;

b    some recruitment;

c    the taking of steps to improve employee morale and motivation?

21    Can redundancy be used to:

a    link pay to performance; (pp. 64–5)

b    improve the management structure (e.g. by reducing the number of levels); (p. 41)

c    alter bargaining arrangements, where there is a union, to reflect the changes in 21 (a) and 21 (b) above? (pp. 24–5)

22    Do any of the proposed changes involve alterations to the terms of contracts of employment and if so, how can such changes be implemented with the minimum risk of legal challenge? (pp. 63–4)

# *Appendix II*
## European Community Directives on Redundancy[1]

The 1975 directive required Member States to enact legislation placing duties on employers to consult with workers' representatives where redundancies were contemplated and to notify the appropriate public authorities where redundancies were projected.[2] In Britain, the relevant legislation is to be found in the TULR(C)A.[3] (See above pp. 111–21.)

In some respects the British law is better for the employee than is the minimum required by the 1975 directive – for example, consultation rights are not restricted to situations where there are ten or more redundancies – but in other respects the EC requirements may not have been met fully. In particular, the British legislation reduces the duties of consultation and notification such that where there are special circumstances that render it not reasonably practicable for an employer to fulfil his duties, he must then take 'all such steps . . . as are reasonably practicable'.[4] Moreover, the 1975 directive seems to envisage that the period following notification would be used by the public authorities to seek solutions to the problem which has given rise to the projected redundancies.[5] There is nothing in the British legislation to require such a role for the public authorities. Another issue is the limitation (in British law but not in the directive) of consultation rights to situations in which an independent trades union is recognized. This is the basis of European Commission infringement proceedings against the UK. As collective bargaining declines in its coverage the application of the consultation rights diminishes.[6] A further factor is the requirement that an employer must be 'proposing' redundancy (which has been interpreted to mean that the employer must have specific plans: see pp. 113–14) whereas the directive uses the word 'contemplating'.[7] In *Dansk Metalarbejderforbund and Specialarbejder-forbundet i Danmark* v. *H. Nielsen and Son Maskinfabrik A/S (in liquidation)* the Advocate General was of the opinion that contemplating meant an earlier stage than that at which redundancies were planned.

The European Commission has already charged other Member States with failure to implement the 1975 directive. In *Commission of the European Communities* v. *Belgium*, the ECJ held that domestic legislation which did not require employers to provide information, including the number of redundancies and the time-scale, and which did not lay down a 30-day waiting period, did not comply with the directive. In *Commission of the European Communities* v. *Italy*, first in June 1982 and then in November 1985, the ECJ held that Italy was in breach of its Treaty obligations by failure to implement the directive. The defence – that socio-economic conditions were not suitable – was rejected.

Perhaps it is not surprising in the light of the two previous paragraphs that the European Community has adopted a further directive on collective redundancies.[8] This strengthens the original 1975 provisions by requiring that:

- consultation must be in good time and must cover social measures designed to mitigate the effects of redundancy;
- information must be provided in good time and must include the proposed selection criteria, the categories of worker to be made redundant and the method of calculating extra-statutory RPs;
- consultation and information must still be provided even where the redundancy decision is taken by some controlling body rather than the employer, and that this is not to be taken as a defence;
- termination by judicial decision-making is now included; and
- a remedy must be available where the provisions are breached.

Member States must implement the new directive by 24 June 1994.[9]

## Notes

1 75/129 of 17 February 1975 (OJ, 1975 L48) and 56/92 of 24 June 1992 (OJ, 1992 L245).
2 Art. 2.
3 TULR(C)A, ss. 188–98. As already noted, the TURERA seeks to deal with areas in which UK legislation is thought not to implement the directive, for example, by not specifying: that consultation must be with a view to agreement; that it should cover ways of avoiding or minimizing redundancies; and that it should seek to mitigate the effects of redundancy.
4 TULR(C)A, ss. 188(7) and 193(7). However, the TURERA provides that lack of information from a controlling, parent company will not provide a special circumstances defence.
5 Art. 4.
6 On the reduced spread of collective bargaining see Millward, N., Stevens, M., Smart, D. and Hawes, W., *Workplace Industrial Relations in Transition*, Aldershot: Dartmouth Publishing, 1992.
7 Art. 2; TULR(C)A, s. 188(1).

8 Council Directive 92/56 of 24 June 1992 amending Directive 75/129 on the Approximation of the Laws of the Member States Relating to Collective Redundancies (OJ, 1992 L245).

9 In the absence of full implementation through domestic law a complainant may rely, depending upon the circumstances, on the directive itself or an interpretation of domestic law which accords with it. Moreover, a Member State is obliged to make good the damage suffered by individuals as a result of its failure to implement a directive.

# List of Statutes, Statutory Instruments and European Community Sources

## Statutes

# Statutory Instruments

## European Community Sources

# List of Cases

# Bibliography

Advisory, Conciliation and Arbitration Service, *Employment Handbook*, London: ACAS, 1990.
—— *Labour Flexibility in Britain: The 1987 ACAS Survey*, Occasional Paper 41, London: ACAS, 1988.
—— *Redundancy Arrangements: The 1986 ACAS Survey*, Occasional Paper 37, London: ACAS, 1987.
—— *Redundancy Handling*, Advisory Booklet number 12, London: ACAS, 1989.
BCE Outplacement, *Customised Outplacement Programmes*, Mansfield: BCE Ltd, 1992.
Benson, E., *A Guide to Redundancy Law*, London: MacMillan, 1985.
Bird, D., Redundancies in Great Britain, *Employment Gazette*, pp. 459–63, London: HMSO, August 1991.
Booth, A.L., Extra-Statutory Redundancy Payments in Britain, *British Journal of Industrial Relations*, November 1987.
Bourn, C., *Redundancy Law and Practice*, London: Butterworths, 1983.
Brown, W., (Ed.) *The Changing Contours of British Industrial Relations*, Oxford: Basil Blackwell, 1981.
Burrows, G., *Redundancy Counselling for Managers*, London: Institute of Personnel Management, 1985.
Croner Publications Ltd, *Croner's Europe*, Volume 1, pp. 2–751 ff (Employment Law and The Single Market), Kingston upon Thames: Croner Publications Ltd, 1992.
Cross, M., (Ed.) *Managing Workforce Reduction*, London: Croom Helm, 1985.
Cross, M., *Towards the Flexible Craftsman*, London: Technical Change Centre, 1985.
Coulson-Thomas, C. and Coe, T., *The Flat Organization: Philosophy and Practice*, British Institute of Management, 1991.
Daniel, W.W. and Millward, N., *Workplace Industrial Relations in Britain*, London: Heinemann, 1983.

Daniel, W.W., *Whatever Happened to the Workers in Woolwich?*, Broadsheet No. 537, London: Political and Economic Planning, 1972.

Department of Employment, *Industrial Relations Code of Practice*, London: HMSO, 1972.

—— *Redundancy Payments*, Employment Legislation Series, No. 16, London: DE, 1991.

Department of Employment and Productivity, *Dealing with Redundancies*, London: Department of Employment and Productivity, 1968.

Dey, I.F., A study of the formulation and implementation of policies relating to redundancy and unemployment by the AUEW District Committee, Bristol, 1970–72, Ph.D. thesis, University of Bristol, 1979.

Donovan, Lord, *Report on Trades Unions and Employers' Associations 1965–68*, Cmnd 3623, London: HMSO, 1968.

Dunn, S. and Gennard, J., *The Closed Shop in British Industry*, London: MacMillan, 1984.

Economist Publications Ltd, *Managing Redundancies*, London: Economist Publications, 1985.

Edwards, P., Marginson, P., Purcell, J. and Sisson, K., *The Management of Industrial Relations in Large Enterprises*, Warwick Papers in Industrial Relations, No. 11, Coventry: University of Warwick, 1991.

Eldridge, J.E.T., *Industrial Disputes*, London: Routledge and Kegan Paul, 1968.

Flanders, A., *Collective Bargaining: Prescription for Change*, London: Faber and Faber, 1967.

Flynn, J., *Managing Redundancy*, London: Croom Helm, 1985.

Freeman, R.B. and Medoff, J.L., *What do Trades Unions do?*, New York: Basic Books Inc., 1984, p. 109.

Gennard, J., *Job Security and Industrial Relations*, Paris, Organization for Economic Co-operation and Development, 1979.

Gordon, A., *Redundancy in the 1980s*, Aldershot: Gower Publishing, 1984.

Guest, D.E., Human Resource Management and Industrial Relations, *Journal of Management Studies*, 24, 5, 503–22.

Grunfeld, C., *The Law of Redundancy*, 3rd edition, London: Sweet & Maxwell, 1989.

Hardy, C., *Managing Organization Closure*, Aldershot: Gower Publishing, 1985.

Harris, C.C., *Redundancy and Recession*, Oxford: Basil Blackwell, 1987.

Health and Safety Commission, Oil Industry Advisory Committee, *Guidance on Multi-Skilling in the Petroleum Industry*, London: HMSO, 1992.

Herron, F., *Labour Market in Crisis*, London: MacMillan, 1975.

Hunter, L.C., Reid, G.L. and Boddy, D., *Labour Problems of Technical Change*, London: George Allen & Unwin, 1970.

Incomes Data Services, *Redundancy*, Handbook 51, London: IDS, 1991.

—— *Redundancy Terms*, Study 464, London: IDS, 1990.

—— *Managing Redundancy*, Study 511, London: IDS, 1992.

Industrial Relations Services, *Employment Trends*, 495, London: IRS, September 1991, pp. 7–10 (Job Security Agreements in the US Motor Industry).

—— *Industrial Relations Review and Report*, 409, London: IRS, 2 February 1988, pp. 2–9 (Redundancy Pay 1988).

Inland Revenue, *Ex Gratia Awards Made on Termination of an Office or Employment by Retirement or Death*, Statement of Practice SP 13/91, London: Inland Revenue, 1991.

Institute of Manpower Studies, *Corporate Employment Policies and the Older Worker*, Brighton: IMS, 1991.

—— *Redundancy Provisions Survey*, IMS Commentary No. 13, Brighton: IMS, 1981.

Institute of Personnel Management, *The IPM Redundancy Code*, London: IPM, 1991.

Jahoda, Lazarsfeld and Zeisel, *Marienthal*, London: Tavistock Publications, 1972.

Jones, K., *The Human Face of Change*, London: IPM, 1974.

Kahn, H., *Repercussions of Redundancy*, London: Allen & Unwin, 1964.

Kemp, F., Buttle, B. and Kemp, D., *Coping with Redundancy*, London: Kogan Page, 1981.

Lee, R.M., (Ed.) *Redundancy, Lay-offs and Plant Closures*, London: Croom Helm, 1987.

Lee, R.M., The Entry to Self-Employment of Redundant Steelworkers, *Industrial Relations Journal*, 16, 2, 42–9, 1985.

Lewis, P., *Practical Employment Law: A Guide for Human Resource Managers*, Oxford: Blackwell, 1992.

MacKay, D.I., MacKay, R., McVean, P. and Edwards, R., *Redundancy and Displacement*, DE Research Paper, No. 16, London: DE, 1980.

Martin, R. and Fryer, R.H., Management and Redundancy: An Analysis of Planned Organizational Change, *British Journal of Industrial Relations*, VIII, 1, 69–84, 1970.

Martin, R., and Wallace, J., *Working Women in Recession*, Oxford: Oxford University Press, 1984.

McMullen, J., *Business Transfers and Employee Rights*, 2nd edition, London: Butterworths, 1992.

Millward, N. and Stevens, M., *British Workplace Industrial Relations 1980–84*, Aldershot: Gower Publishing, 1986.

Millward, N., Stevens, M., Smart, D. and Hawes, W., *Workplace Industrial Relations in Transition*, Aldershot: Dartmouth Publishing, 1992.

Morris, L.D., Patterns of Social Activity and Post-Redundancy Labour Market Experience, *Sociology*, 18, 3 (August 1984).

Mukherjee, S., *Through No Fault of Their Own*, London: MacDonald, 1973.

Mumford, P., *Redundancy and Security of Employment*, Farnborough: Gower Publishing, 1975.

Noble, I., Walker, A. and Westergaard, J., *After Redundancy: The Experience of Economic Insecurity*, Polity Press, 1986.

Parker, S.R., Thomas, C.G., Ellis, N.D. and McCarthy, W.E.J., *Effects of the Redundancy Payments Act*, London: HMSO, 1971.

Public Accounts Committee, *Report of an Inquiry into Redundancy Schemes for University Staffs*, London: HMSO, 1986.

Smith, A.D., *Redundancy Practices in Four Countries*, Paris: OECD, 1966.

Storey, J. (Ed.) *New Perspectives on Human Resource Management*, London: Routledge, 1991.

Thomas, R. (Ed.) *An Exercise in Redeployment*, Oxford: Pergamon, 1969.

Towers, B., (Ed.) *A Handbook of Industrial Relations Practice*, 3rd edition, London: Kogan Page, 1992.

—— *The Handbook of Human Resource Management*, Oxford: Blackwell, 1992.

Turnbull, P.J., Leaner and Possibly Fitter: The Management of Redundancy in Britain, *Industrial Relations Journal*, 19, 3, 201–13, 1988.

Upex, R., (General Editor), *Encyclopedia of Employment Law*, London: Sweet & Maxwell, 1992.

Wedderburn, D., *White Collar Redundancy*, Cambridge: Cambridge University Press, 1964.

—— *Redundancy and the Railwaymen*, Cambridge: Cambridge University Press, 1965.

White, P., The Management of Redundancy, *Industrial Relations Journal*, 14, 1, 32–40, 1983.

Withington, J., *Shutdown – Anatomy of a Shipyard Closure*, London: Bedford Square Press, 1989.

Wood, S. and Cohen, S., Approaches to the Study of Redundancy, *Industrial Relations Journal*, 8, 4 (1977–8).

Wood, S. and Dey, I., *Redundancy*, Aldershot: Gower Publishing, 1983.

Yemin, E., (Ed.) *Workforce Reductions in Undertakings*, Geneva: International Labour Office, 1982.

# Index